He with Faith, Friendship and Love

The True Story of a Stroke Survivor
A Born Dreamer

B.S. Kesavan M.D.

INDIA · SINGAPORE · MALAYSIA

Notion Press

Old No. 38, New No. 6
McNichols Road, Chetpet
Chennai - 600 031

First Published by Notion Press 2018
Copyright © B.S. Kesavan 2018
All Rights Reserved.

ISBN 978-1-64324-692-5

Contents

Acknowledgments

My true story is born out of my unrelenting determination to seek the truth about who I am. I was born as an innocent little one, and then grew up as a carefree, joyful and restless guy, and later became a much more focused person in life. During this journey, I also found the resilience to overcome rough patches in life. Faith, friendship and love helped me to survive in this treacherous world. Unbelievable courage helped me to get past all the obstacles I encountered and overcome rising tides to achieve success in life. Untimely illness did not deter me the ability to keep going.

I have to thank Dr. Marc Katchen, my neurologist, for his initial encouragement to write my story. I also want to thank Jim Jacobs for giving me ideas about how to write this book. My sincere thanks to my wonderful transcriptionist Lois and her loving husband John. Because of their hospitality, I was able to write this book without any stress. With love and empathy, I am very thankful for all my friends and family with whom I am undertaking this unending life's journey now. I am very thankful to Notion Press for accepting my writing and agreeing to publish this book. I also appreciate the senior publishing consultant at Notion, Mr. Manikandan, for his guidance and support. I also appreciate the project manager, Gabriela Caster, for continuous support and help with this endeavor.

I am thankful to my parents who shared their DNA, so that I could carry on their memory in my story. Thank you, mom and dad. I am thankful for my siblings, who gave me their unconditional love while I was growing up. I am very grateful to my coworkers for helping me to become a good physician. I am extremely proud of the young, vibrant _God's angels'— the children for whom I was caring for while I was in practice. They are the priceless treasures, the _pearls' in my life. Finally, I want to thank my dear family, my wife, my son and daughter-in-law, my daughter and son-in-law for their unconditional love and support. I am eternally thankful to the Almighty God for giving me four wonderful grandchildren. They are the joy of my life. Now, I have found a new pathway to travel and that path is leading me to my spiritual journey.

Thank you all.

Introduction

Life is a beautiful journey, in which we all go through ups and downs. Life is like a game – but it is not about winning or losing; it is about doing our best. Success relates to a happy life, and a happy life is just a string of happy moments.

My story begins with my Creator, whom I call _Shakti'. I also refer to my Creator as _Amma' (_mother' in Tamil, my mother tongue). I developed firm faith in myself, and strong hope for a better future. All of this helped me to overcome my sufferings. I consider success and suffering as the two sides of a coin. I believe that, if you have strong faith in yourself and your Creator, you will always find a way to overcome tribulations.

I also believe in strong roots—even though I came from a different country, at a different time, from a different culture. I believe that my story will help future generations to understand more about their roots.

This story is also about healing of the mind and body with the help of faith, friendship and love, while battling a major illness. It is about how will power can help overcome difficulties with grace. Resilience and optimism helped me to heal myself with flying colors. My innate ability to dream helped to build my hope for a better future. Thus, I selected the title of this book: *Healing the Mind with Faith, Friendship and Love: The True Story of a Stroke Survivor A Born Dreamer*.

I was born a dreamer; I still dream. Some of my dreams have come true, and some are still up in the air. With help from my Creator, I am going to write my story the way I remember it.

Chapter One

4TH OF JULY WEEKEND 2016: WHAT A SURPRISE!

May all be peaceful, happy and light in body and spirit,
May all be safe and free from injury,
May all be free from fear, anxiety, anger and
afflictions.

—Thich Nhat Hanh

Appreciation of others and appreciation of one's self are the closest vibrational matches to the source energy of everything we have ever witnessed, anywhere in this universe. A surprise was in store for me on the weekend of July 4, 2016. That weekend was very special to us: Two weeks earlier, our daughter-in-law had given birth to our second, very beautiful, granddaughter—on Father's Day, and it was my gift on that day. My son, a pediatric gastroenterologist who works at Rush Medical Center, lives in Chicago with his family. My daughter-in-law is an allergy specialist in private practice.

I had had a plan for that weekend, but my Shakti had a different plan for me. Until that moment, I felt I was invincible and nothing could happen to me. In the early morning of July 3, everything in my life turned upside-down.

On July 1st, a Friday, I finished a full day of work at my office (I was a pediatrician), seeing my wonderful patients, whom I consider my own children, and rested well that night. July 2nd was just like any other Saturday, except that it was the beginning of the three-day-long weekend for Independence Day. On Saturday morning, I went for my walk as usual. I have been a walker for most of my life, and this habit helps to release stress. The weather was beautiful—the sun was shining, birds were singing, the trees were very green, and there was a pleasant breeze. My wife and I decided to travel to Chicago that same day by the noon train. The train left two hours late, so we reached Chicago that evening. My son picked us up and took us to his home. Our daughter-in-law greeted us at the doorstep along with our 21-month-old granddaughter. She called me _Thatha' or _Grandpa' in my native language. We had taught our granddaughter to call us _Thatha' and _Patti'. Inside, we saw our two-week-old granddaughter for the first time.

We had a wonderful dinner and nice conversation, and I went to bed at around nine or nine-thirty p.m. I fell asleep immediately and slept without any disturbance. I felt good because the train journey had been excellent, and seeing my granddaughters made me very happy. Around five-thirty a.m. the next day—July 3rd—I woke up. Suddenly, I was finding it difficult to speak. I wanted to say something, but the words would not come out. I also noticed that I was unable to swallow my saliva. I was puzzled. What was going on? I needed to use the bathroom, which was next to our bedroom. I slowly struggled to get up from the bed when, all of a sudden, I felt my right hand fall flat. Oh my god! I tried to say something but only a babble of sounds came through. My wife stirred as she was still half asleep and whispered something softly as she did not want to wake up our granddaughter, who was sleeping in the room across the hallway from our bedroom. I tried to say something to my wife but no words emerged from my mouth. I tried to stand slowly. Then, I noticed my right leg felt very weak and I had no strength to move. At that time, I did not realize what was going on and dragged my feet slowly towards the door. I tried to open the door with my right hand but my right hand was very weak and kept falling down, so I could not open it. During these attempts, I made some noise and my wife again whispered that I should not disturb our granddaughter. I was helpless at that moment! After a great struggle, I opened the door with my left hand and slowly dragged my feet and entered the bathroom. All of a sudden, I fell down with a loud crash. Luckily, I fell on the carpet and did not suffer any head injury. Even when I fell down flat, I was moaning and murmuring but no words came out. This was the fourth time in my life that I felt I was near death—it was a very strange feeling and I did not know what to do. Soon, my son and my wife both came to the bathroom and saw me on the floor. My son immediately recognized what was going on and called 911. A fire truck came within a few minutes; the ambulance came 20 minutes later. This was relayed to me by my wife and son later on. When I was on the floor, I was still conscious but my mind was in panic mode and I was wondering what was going on. I remembered that I was carried to the ambulance after they put in an IV line for hydration. Then I remembered that the ambulance was on the way to the hospital. My son preferred that the ambulance take me to Rush Medical Center, where he works, since it is a comprehensive neurological center but that was a 30-minute drive from his home. The ambulance driver preferred to take me to the nearest hospital, which was within 10 minutes from his home. While I was in the ambulance, I had no idea who was accompanying me but I had a vague understanding that I was going to the hospital. I realized that I was having a stroke.

Before the stroke happened, I was an active pediatric practitioner in a rural Midwestern town. I was with a four-member pediatric group and we were all very well liked by our patients. I had faced many challenges, and several difficulties and surprises throughout my life, but I had had the ability to overcome each and every challenge with a strong faith in my Creator, my Shakti.

When I was just 21 years old, and was in medical school, I underwent a very painful experience that robbed me of my happiness for a while. Until then, I was a very carefree, happy person; nothing ever bothered me. The sad thing that happened was the loss of my beloved, wonderful dad, due to lung cancer. That was a terrible loss for me because I loved my dad and admired him. He was a good, honest and spiritual man. He was the first person I had admired and loved, and lost forever. At that time, my classmate (who was older than me) helped me to deal with the difficult situation. He was my best friend, and I considered him my older brother. He gave me unconditional love and affection, and I am very thankful to him. Thus, I was able to overcome my sorrow and early depression. Losing my father put a spoke in my life's journey but, because of my inner strength, faith in my Shakti and my friend's unconditional love and support, I withstood the challenge.

Chapter Two

MY UNEXPECTED STAY IN THE HOSPITAL AS A PATIENT

Variety causes contemplation. Contemplation produces preference. Preference is asking. Asking is always answered.

—Esther Hicks

I remembered that I was rushed to the Emergency Room, where I was surrounded by young, very caring people. It was early morning and I vaguely remember being taken for a CT scan of the head. When I was brought back to the Emergency Room, I opened my eyes and I saw my son and wife standing in the doorway. I then noticed my son's best friend, who is a stroke specialist at the hospital where my son works. I tried to tell them something—and, to my surprise, a few words came through. I was thrilled! Then, I tried to raise my right hand, and was able to raise it halfway. Also, I noticed that I was able to move my right leg with ease, so I was really excited. By the time all this happened, my loved ones came around me and began to encourage me. I felt that I was recovering quickly. I was later told that the CT scan showed a blood clot in the middle cerebral artery; by the time I had another CT angiogram of the head, the blood clot had disappeared! I call this a miracle. I have no explanation but I have deep faith in my Shakti as the cause of such an event.

Upon my admission to the hospital, my son had informed my daughter and nephews, who are living in different parts of the United States. He also informed my colleagues, and made sure that my hospital knew what was happening.

From the Emergency Room, I was moved to the hospital as they decided to keep me for observation. I was admitted to the ninth floor, which was supposed to be a neuro unit. I was to share the room with another person. I was not able to see him because of the curtain between us, but the constant noise from the television and loud sounds coming from the oxygen machine (connected to my roommate) made it very difficult to rest. Vital signs taken every thirty minutes by the nursing staff added to the difficulty.

During this time, one of my best friends from my hometown paid me a visit with his wife (on the morning of July 3rd), and I am still very grateful to them for that act of kindness. To their surprise, I was repeating *mantras* (spiritual words or chants) in Sanskrit.

In all, I was unable to get the rest I needed. First, I saw the medical resident on call that day; later, I saw the attending doctor on call. Since this was a holiday weekend, the neurologist did not show up until late in the evening. To my surprise, she spent very little time examining me, and asked me only a few questions. After that, I saw her dictating notes, which took longer than my examination. My son asked her if she would call his friend, the stroke specialist, but she declined. That night, I was constantly disturbed because of the noise of the TV and the sound of the oxygen machine running. I was also awakened throughout the night for checking of vital signs.

On the morning of July 4th, at about four a.m., the nurse came in and shut off the TV—which was a big relief. A little while later, my co-patient was discharged; I was extremely relieved. My wife stayed with me; my son and his best friend, the stroke specialist, were my first visitors. I am very thankful to her because it was her weekend off and she was not on call at this hospital. I was told later that she had rushed to the hospital as soon as I was admitted to the emergency room. My son knew her from their school days at Illinois Math and Science Academy (IMSA) in Aurora, Illinois; they both went to medical school together at University of Illinois at the Peoria Medical School as well. She had gone on to Boston to do a fellowship in neurology and had further specialized in stroke. My son went to Columbia University in New York for pediatric training and then pediatric gastroenterology. He then went to Cornell University in New York as an attending for two years in pediatric gastroenterology, before moving to Rush Medical Center in Chicago.

On seeing all my loved ones around me on the morning of July 4th, I felt much better and was able to express myself more clearly. I was able to send text messages, which made me feel more confident about my recovery. I even texted my family doctor and my office nurse that I was doing well.

The physical therapist came in and asked me a few questions about how I was doing. I said I was doing okay, so he told me to sit up on the bed. With a little difficulty, I was able to do so. Then, he asked me to raise my upper arm. Suddenly, my right arm felt very weak. I was also unable to speak—I lost my voice and my right leg fell down and was limp. I could see that my wife, son and his friend were visibly shaken by this development. Tears were flowing down from my son's eyes.

They immediately rushed me to the radiology department and I had another CT scan of the head. On the way back to the floor, I slowly regained my voice, and strength in my right lower leg and right upper arm. On seeing what was happening, and disappointed with the care I was being given at this facility, my son and his friend decided that I should be transferred to Rush Medical Center—more so since it is a comprehensive neurological unit. They discussed this with the doctors, and they all agreed that it would a better place for my care. Therefore, arrangements were made for my transfer.

Off I went in another ambulance ride to another hospital. This drive was not very difficult. It took around 30 minutes but it was comfortable, and I was fully conscious, knowing exactly what was going on. By noon on July 4th, I reached Rush Medical Center. The neuro unit, I heard, was built very recently and it looked excellent. I was given a beautiful private room on the twelfth floor. There was no TV in the room—so, I was even more relieved. They even provided an extra bed for my wife. Since July 4th was a holiday, I first saw the medical intern on call; he performed a good exam. Later, I saw my wife, son and his best friend (the stroke specialist) entering the room. All of this encouraged me a lot. When the stroke specialist said that everything would be fine, I felt much better. She added that her neurology chief was going to be my attending physician, and he would be seeing me the next day. However, I still had no definite idea of what was going on; even though the situation was stressful, I felt at peace. I felt that my Shakti was with me—as long as She was with me, I was going to be fine.

Chapter Three

THE PARADISE LAND; MY HUMBLE BEGINNING

Happy moments, praise God; difficult moments, seek God, quiet moments, worship God; painful moments, trust God; every moment, thank God.

—Rick Warren

Happiness, fulfillment and purpose in life are all inner concepts. If you don't have inner peace and serenity, then you have nothing.

—Dr. Wayne W. Dyer

While lying in bed, on the night of the 4th of July, I heard fireworks outside. My mind raced back to my previous journey—which had begun when I was born. My journey started in a tiny village, located along the side of the Arabian Sea, in South India. I was born on September 27, 1946—that was the beginning of the _baby boomer' generation. Also, we were the post-World War II generation, as the war had just ended. Our village was very beautiful, and around two hundred people lived in it. Our house was surrounded by tall coconut trees. I also remembered that there were cattle and chickens on our property; there was a well in front of my house, from which we drew water for all uses.

The name of our village was Ammachiyarcoiloor, which means the ‗place of worship‘. A temple was located just a few yards from our house, and a small river flowed behind the temple. The scenery was excellent. I was born into a very loving, wealthy family that was respected and admired by the villagers. My grandfather had earned most of the wealth and, through his inheritance, my father has acquired farmland that included rice paddy fields and coconut groves.

I was the fifth generation in my family. My great-great-grandfather came from a different village. I was told that he had been very poor when he was young, and there was a great drought in his town. So, he, along with his wife, migrated to the tiny village of Ammachiyarcoiloor. He struggled a lot initially and felt helpless. The story goes that, one day, he was so tired and hungry that he stopped to rest in front of the temple and fell into deep sleep. He had a wonderful dream wherein Amman came to him and told him that he was going to do very well from now on and that all his future generations were also going to be successful and prosperous. He suddenly woke up and realized it was just a dream, but truly believed the Goddess‘s prophecy and began to work hard. From then on, our forefathers accumulated substantial wealth and my father inherited the wealth. I heard that my grandfather was a very hardworking and simple man. He died of acute cardiac arrest. At the time of his death, my father was only

11 years old, and he had a brother who was about 10 years older. The brother became a parent figure to my father.

My father was very intelligent, so he was sent to high school in a nearby town. He went on to college to get his Bachelor's degree. My father was the first one to earn a college degree in his entire village. I am very thankful to him, for his inspiration and encouragement to get an education and to do well. He married twice. He lost his first wife due to smallpox; she was pregnant with their child when she died. He worked for a few months for the government and had to be away from his village. After his wife's death, he resigned from the job and came home. My father married my mother seven years after the death of his first wife. He tried to start a business on his own but that did not work out well. For a brief time, he entered politics and ran for election but was unsuccessful. He then quit politics and became a social reformer and began to help his village's people with their needs. During his time, he established a cooperative bank for the village, encouraged the villagers to study well, and positively motivated them towards better life goals.

My mother was a very simple person. She had studied only up to the fourth grade as, at that time, women were not sent to school once they reached the age of menarche. However, my mother was very intelligent and hard working and she would have done well in her life if she had had a good education. She was a strong woman. She performed her duties as a homemaker while my father spent his time helping the villagers. My mother was the only one at home taking care of us. We were a large family with seven children. I was the fourth among seven children and had three older brothers and three younger sisters. I was called Chinna Thambi (_chinna' means _small' and _thambi' means _younger brother') by my dad and my brothers. My mother called me by my real name albeit in a shortened form. My brothers were very protective of me.

My brothers and I always played outside. We had no other social activities, and there was no TV, radio or video games at that time. At the age of 4, I faced my first near-death experience. Before I talk about the experience, I must mention that I was very afraid of the dark, of dogs and going into water. My brothers and their friends used to walk to the river behind the Amman temple to swim and play in the water. I never went with them. One day, my brothers took me along with them and told me to sit by the side of the river; then, they jumped into the river with their friends. The river did not have a powerful current but the water was a bit deep for someone of my age. All of a sudden, I heard a dog barking and, without realizing what I was doing, I jumped into the river. I began to drown. For the first time in my life, I had the feeling that I was going to die—this was my first near-death experience. My brothers did not notice that I was drowning because they were playing with their friends. Suddenly, one of my brother's friends saw me going underwater and he rushed over and pulled me out. I was saved! I was very thankful to him and to Amman, our family deity, for helping me at that critical moment.

Now, I have to tell you a story I heard from our villagers about the origin of our family deity. Around 600 years ago, fishermen found our Amman in the Arabian Sea. At first, they thought it was a big fish but soon found out that it was a deity's statue and brought it to the village. The villagers installed the deity and built a temple. She is our *kula deivam* or family deity.

After that day, when I was rescued from drowning, I have had very deep faith in my Amman or Shakti. Believing in, and having total faith in the Almighty, is my way of prayer. I believe that patience with family is love; patience with others is respect; patience with oneself is confidence; patience with God is faith.

One more thing that I remember is my grandmother's death. When I was close to 5 years old, I remember my grandmother dying very peacefully in our home in my father's lap.

In this context, I have to say a few words about the Hindu religion. No one knows the exact origin of the religion or of who started it. As I was told, it started in the Indus Valley, and is a philosophical religion; it is a way of life. Hindus believe in one Creator who is in an inactive state (or unmanifested state), whom we call him Brahman. When he becomes active (or manifested), we call him Shakti. There are many different gods and goddesses in this religion. Just like the sun is at the center of our solar system, and sends out multiple rays to earth, there is one God but with different names for us to understand the Creator—the only one that is omnipresent and omnipotent. In our customs, each family has their own personal God—for our family, Amman is the family god, but we worship other forms of gods as well. Ultimately, we realize there is only one Creator who protects the entire universe.

Now, I am going to share a few things about our powerful Amman. Herein, I refer to my family deity as Shakti, which means cosmic power. According to Hinduism, the Creator is called Brahman. According to the teachings of Sri Ramakrishna, wherever there is action, such as creation, preservation and destruction, there is Shakti or Intelligent Energy. That one Absolute Existence-Knowledge-Bliss is the external Intelligent Energy that creates, preserves and destroys the universe. When the Supreme Being is thought of as *nishkriya* (inactive)—neither creating, sustaining nor destroying, we call him Brahman or Purusha (the Male Principle). When we think of him as active—creating, sustaining and destroying—we call him Shakti, Maya or Prakriti (the Female Principle). Really speaking, the distinction between Brahman and Shakti is a distinction without a difference. They are one—just like fire and its burning power; as milk and its white hue; as a gem and its brightness. You cannot conceive one without the other.

I have to tell you about the other activities, besides playing outside, which we indulged in when we were young. We used to go the seashore and collect seashells, bring them home and keep them as a trophy. We also used to build sand mountains and roll over on them. It was a beautiful experience.

I was educated in my village only up to the first grade. After that, we moved to a nearby town for better education. The teacher I had in the first grade was very nice and good but very strict as well. She liked me and expected a lot from me; I did well at that early age. My teacher and mother were good friends, and my teacher told my mother about what was going on in school. Once, she told my mother, ―This boy needs a lot of appreciation and praise. If you appreciate him more, he will do a lot better. You can bet one crore rupees on him." (Rupee is the name for Indian currency; one crore equals ten million in numeric terms. In currency terms, it is currently equal to about one hundred fifty thousand dollars.) So, from that young age, I knew that I had to do well and that everyone had high expectations of me. I falsely believed that I was the brightest among my siblings, but the truth was that my older brother and younger sister were the brightest people in my family. Even though my brother did not use his skills in education, he did very well in his life. My youngest sister was also very intelligent but, unfortunately after my father's death, she suffered a lot. With good support and care from her husband, she is also doing very well. I am very thankful to my Amman, my Shakti, who looks after all my family members as her own children.

Another memory that comes to mind is of my sister, who was just two years younger than me. When she was 2 years old, she fell gravely ill and was treated by a native doctor who was not medically trained. At that time, she was the only sister we had. She was so ill that she was almost semiconscious. By our Amman's grace, we came to know of another doctor, who was visiting our village from a nearby town. My father asked him to come and see my sister. The doctor diagnosed my sister as having typhoid fever and gave her the medicine needed for her recovery. Her recovery was a miracle. Later, she got married and had three wonderful children. Unfortunately, she died of breast cancer at the age of 59. This was the third major loss from among my dear ones.

Coming back to the present, it was the evening of July 4th. I was better rested but was still awakened every two hours for vital signs. However, I felt much better than the previous day. I could hardly wait to meet my neurologist the next morning, and to see what his evaluation would reveal.

In the meantime, my wife told me that my daughter and her family had arrived in Chicago and they were coming to see me the next day. I was very excited and eager to see my daughter and her family, but hospital rules do not allow children under 12 to visit. So, I was unable to see my grandchildren aged 3 and (almost) 1 but was fortunately able to see my loving daughter and son-in-law. I am really thankful for their concern and compassion.

My daughter went for her undergraduate education at Illinois Wesleyan in Bloomington, Illinois, and post-graduate education at Sarah Lawrence at Bronxville, New York, for creative writing. Before her children were born, she was a special education teacher. Now, with two young children, she is a stay-at-home mom. My son-in-law is a wonderful human being—always positive and pleasant, and very hard working. He did his undergraduate schooling at New York University, New York City, then received his Masters in computer science at Stanford University, California. He also received his law degree from Berkeley, California. Now he is working for a software company in Silicon Valley. He comes from a wonderful family, and they all live close to him. I am very fortunate to be surrounded by a very loving family—everything is given by Amman, my Shakti, and I am very thankful.

Chapter Four

HAPPY MOMENTS DURING SCHOOL DAYS

No person or power in the outside world can compare to the power you have within. You seek the power within as it knows the perfect way for you.
—Rhonda Byrne

The mind is everything. What you think, you become.
—Gautama Buddha

In human life, there is no security or certainty. They are the two major delusions that we believe as true.
—Eckhart Tolle

Real life is just like a play. We have been given a role to enact. Once it is done, we are gone from the play—that is the fact of life's journey. The world believes that certainty is a state that we can achieve, maintain and hold on to. Also, we believe that having some sort of security is going to make us happy. In reality, however, these two notions are myths, and we are living in a world that believes in false conclusions.

Coming back to my condition. I was lying in bed at the Rush Medical Center in the early hours of July 5th, anxiously waiting to see my daughter and my son-in-law. In the meantime, my mind wandered back to the good old days, when I was a young child. As I had mentioned before, I studied up to first grade in my village; after that, my father decided that we would move to a nearby town, 5 km from our village, for us to benefit from better education. Now I realize and appreciate what a thoughtful decision that was. Thank you, dad.

Most of the towns are named after famous temples located there. The town we moved to got its name—Nagercoil—from the Nagaraja Temple there (‗naga‘ means snake, and ‗raja‘ means king; the full word refers to a king cobra). I was enrolled at a Christian mission elementary school until the fifth grade. My only memory I have of that time is of walking to school. I usually walked with the oldest of my younger sisters. It took us 10 to 15 minutes to reach the school, and the roads were very narrow. It was very safe to walk because the traffic was very less when compared to present day. After finishing the fifth grade, I went to Sethu Lakshmi Bai High School (we called it S.L.B. High School), which was named after a famous queen called Sethu Lakshmi Bai. Back then, we entered a six-year period in high school. After finishing the eleventh grade, we did one year of college (called pre-university) before we selected our professional school.

India is, as you know, a subcontinent—just like Europe. India obtained independence from British rule in 1947. Before that, we were ruled by different kingdoms with varying cultures. The British ruled India for almost 300 years, and all native kingdoms were under British control. Our kingdom had also been under British control.

While in the sixth grade, I had some difficulty acquiring math skills but I was very good in English, history and science. I started learning English as a second language once I entered the sixth grade and continued until I finished high school; once you entered college, the medium of instruction was mainly English. I still remember my math teacher—he was very strict. If any students did not do well in his class, he would punish them by knocking their heads against the wall. I was very determined to do well, so I studied very hard and, thankfully, never got punished.

From a young age, I loved to compete, and always wanted to excel and do better than the next person. I always dreamt of becoming a great person someday. Because of my family's encouragement and expectation, even though my dad and mom never pushed me to study hard, I felt I should work hard and study well. My father was a successful farmer but he never took any of us to see his properties as he did not want us to be influenced by his wealth. His mantra was that a good education would bring about a better future. He periodically went back to the village to take care of his land, and I remember returning to our home in the village during school holidays.

During my school days, I made friends with children with different faiths. India has a large Hindu population with ethnic minorities of Christian, Muslim, Jewish and Parsi faiths, and we all lived together, harmoniously. Nagercoil had a sizeable Christian population, and there is a famous church where I attended some weddings.

I had a friend and classmate who had the same last name as mine—Kesavan. My name has two parts—Shanmuga Kesavan. Shanmuga is one of the names of a god named Muruga. Kesavan is one of the thousand names of a god named Vishnu. It was a very sad moment for me when I learned that Kesavan had passed away.

It is interesting to note that, in our tradition, children keep their father's name as their first initial—so, my original name was B. (Brahmanandswamy) Shanmuga Kesavan. Girls, however, changed it to their husband's name after they got married.

One of my good habits I developed while in school was a love for reading. I loved to go to the library; I would walk because my father did not have a car. I liked all my teachers but there was one teacher I was especially fond of—he taught us Tamil in the final year of high school. He encouraged me to enter a writing competition, representing my school for the school district. I initially had strong reservations but finally agreed to enter the competition because of his consistent encouragement. To my surprise, I was selected as the best writer in the whole school district! I am very thankful to my teacher for encouraging me at a young age. I also really liked my English teacher; he used to talk about poetry, most of which were written by British poets. I remember Wordsworth from his poem about daffodils, and the meaning of that poem. Another teacher who really inspired me was my social studies teacher. She was a wonderful human being. She used to borrow my book sometimes for her preparation for class. When we were leaving school, we got autographs from our teachers. She wrote two words— _Aim high'—which inspired me to dream big for my future. Back then, at the age of 15, I did not really understand the meaning of the words but they kept my dream alive.

At the start of the ninth grade, I fell very sick and was kept home for nearly a month. My whole body was swollen and I was on bed rest. I was later told that both my kidneys were infected due to Strep. By the grace of my Amman, I recovered without any long-term, residual side effects. I was kept on a low-salt diet for one month. I craved salt at that time but the doctor told my mother my diet should be salt-free. Later, I developed the habit of not adding much salt to my food; thinking back, that has been a big benefit.

I do not remember being vaccinated for childhood diseases such as measles or mumps, as well as diphtheria, whooping cough or polio. I remember having had measles and mumps.

After our move to the new town, and after school hours, I used to play outside with my friends since, as I said before, we did not have television or video games; however, now we had a small radio set and liked to hear music, which was our only entertainment at home.

I wish to share a very painful secret from my school days. I have kept it to myself my whole life, even though I occasionally think about it. Now, I have to talk about it. When I was in high school, I was sexually assaulted by a few of my brother's good friends. I was very innocent and did not know what was going on. I did not have the courage to tell my brothers that their own friends were assaulting me. Luckily, by the grace of my Amman, it did not last long and I soon overcame that very sad incident. However, that painful incident left a permanent scar in my heart. When I became a pediatrician and had to deal with children who were sexually abused, I remembered what happened to me. I was very kind to those children and prayed to my Amman that they should be protected. The one lesson I gained from this experience is that these things are very common—be it in the present time or olden days—but we do not have the courage to tell our parents or our older siblings about them. I think it is better to teach our children from a young age to be open with their parents and share _secrets' that make them uncomfortable. That is the advice I have always given to my patients to guide them to be strong and positive.

When I was young most of my study was done in the early morning hours before I went to school. My mom was an early riser; she woke up at around four a.m. to start preparing breakfast for the whole family and begin on other household chores. My father and I were also early risers. I was the only one among my siblings who woke up early. My father liked to go to the Nagaraja Temple in the morning hours; I also developed the habit of starting my day by paying a visit to the temple, which was about a mile and a half from my house. So, I walked almost three miles every morning. Though my dad and I did not visit this temple at the same time every day, I did, on some occasions, go with my dad to visit other temples in our district. After my early morning *puja* (prayer), I felt so good that I was able to concentrate well on my studies.

When entering the ninth grade, we were required to choose the courses that would help in our future profession. Medicine was regarded as a noble profession and I wanted to be part of it. In those days, it was very hard to get into medical school. The next choices were engineering, agriculture, law and commerce. My two older brothers went to engineering school. By the time I went to the ninth grade, my oldest brother had finished engineering school and begun working. My second oldest brother was still in engineering college. My third brother, who was four years elder to me, had elected to go to medical school due my dad's urging. When I reached the final year of high school, he was attending a very expensive, private medical school. So, when I entered ninth grade, my father preferred that I take up commerce in the future but I wanted to study medicine, too. My father felt that he could not afford to send two children to medical school at the same time. So, I was very angry and jealous. If my father could send my brother to medical school, why not me? I was a bit rebellious at that time, and I challenged my father. I told him I wanted to go to medical school, like my brother. His preference was I should get a Bachelor's degree in commerce, and then join government service (that was what he had done, but quit later). I told my father, ―I am going to study well, get good grades and go to medical school." The wonderful thing about my father was that he always listened to us, even if he did not agree with us. So, finally, he said, ―If you are willing to go down that route, it is fine with me." Thus, I dreamt of becoming a doctor.

In the final year of school (eleventh grade), I was doing quite well. One of my classmates, however, was doing better than me, and I wanted to compete with him. So, I worked harder. At the end of the school year, he was the first in our class and I was second.

After finishing our final year of school, we had to do one more year in college, which was called ‚Pre-university', before choosing our professional school. At that time, there were two colleges in our town. One was within walking distance from my home. When I was finishing high school, our house was being constructed and my dad needed my help in supervising the construction. Fate (or my destiny) went on a different course. The expenses for the local college were also much less, so my dad preferred this. I just agreed to his decision. By that time, my second brother (who was like a father to me) came home from engineering college for vacation. When he looked at my grades, he said, ―Chinna thambi, you are a very intelligent person and your grades are better than all of ours. You do not deserve to go to this college. There is a good college called St. Xavier's College, about 50 miles away from our town. I will take your grades with me and get you admission there." He did not tell our father about his plan for fear that it would make our father very angry. So, he took my grades and went to the school. He presented himself as the real candidate, as they required the presence of the candidate and he (or I) was accepted. Luckily, the school did not find out later that he was not the real candidate. He came home late that night; once my father found out what he had done, he was very upset because he had to spend more money as I would need to stay in the school dorm and other expenses. Finally, he did agree. He would share his opinion but when we reasoned out our stand, he would agree. That was my father's greatness.

Chapter Five

LEAVING MY COMFORT ZONE

*You are the bows from which your children as living
arrows are sent forth. The archer sees the mark upon
the path of the infinite, and He bends you with His
might that His arrows may go swift and far.*

—Khalil Gibran

Coming back to my present state: I was lying in bed in
the early hours of July 5th at Rush Medical Center,
thinking about what the future held for me. I was
waiting for the doctors to come and examine me. I was
anxious to see them. I tried to get up by myself but it
was tough. I slowly got up with my wife's help. I was
trying to stand up, but my right leg felt very weak, and
I had great difficulty using my right hand. Also, my
balance was off. Slowly, with my wife's help, I went to
the bathroom and had my first shower in three days.
Oh, it felt so good! Then, again with my wife's help, I
slowly returned to my room and sat in a chair. This was
the third day after my stroke. I had a very busy
schedule. I was going to see the neurologist for the first
time, as well as the physical therapist and cardiologist.
I was hooked up to all the monitors for my blood

pressure and pulse, and to a Holter monitor for my heartbeat. Now, I was looking like a real patient.

My mind raced back to old days—of the time before I left to attend St. Xavier's College. In the days before I left for the new school, I would argue with my mom for no reason. At one point, even my mom felt that I needed a change. I also felt it was good to leave home to face new challenges. Finally, I arrived at St. Xavier's College for my one year of college before entering medical school. The school was run by Catholic priests; they were very strict. I learned that there was a time to eat, a time to study and a time to socialize. They taught us discipline. The classes were divided into different batches for the preparation of the various professional schools, such as engineering, agriculture, dental/medical, teaching and commerce. My batch, for preparation for medical school, had only 80 students. All my teachers were very nice.

One day, when I was leaving my botany class, I saw one of my fellow classmates. He was looking at a hibiscus flower and doing some research. I was curious to find out what he was doing, so I introduced myself. To my surprise, I found out that he was from the same district, a couple of villages away. We both were also born in the same year, same month and date! From then on, we called ourselves _Birth Mates'. Our friendship is strong even today. I met another friend during our social hours. He was from a different batch, not mine. When we had free time, we would sit together and talk. He introduced me to philosophy.

We had three semesters but only the final semester's grade was counted for getting into medical school. At the end of the first semester, we had exams and our teacher announced the rankings. They read out the ranking, starting from the last of the 80 students in my class. When they read from the last name up to number 10, my name was not there, and I was happy. I found out that I had scored second in my class, so I had only one person better than me. That was a real surprise and I felt very good. I felt that if I worked harder, and believed in my Shakti and myself, I would do very well in the second and final semesters. In the second semester, too, I came in second and the same person came in first. In the third semester, I worked very hard, and hoped to be number one but I had to wait until the final results were reported. In those days, the results were published in the newspaper at a later date, by which time I would be home. Those who achieved the top grades were in the _first class'. A few would be in _second class' but most of them would get _third class'. Some of them would not pass a few subjects, so they would have to repeat the whole year.

Now, I have to tell you about a surprise—a real surprise, even though it started out as a great disappointment. In those days, we did not have computers, telephones or Internet. At the time of our final exam, each student was given a registration number. We were told that the results of our exam would be published in the newspapers, and the date of the announcement of the results would be published a day or two before. The results would come out only after we had gone home for the summer holidays.

So, when I went home, I was very confident and told my dad and brothers that I had done well. I knew that I would excel. Finally, the day of the results came. My dad, as usual, got up early, took a shower and walked to the Nagaraja Temple. After worshiping the deity, he sat around chatting with his friends. He boasted about me, saying that the results are coming, and that ―he is going to do very well". We usually get two sets of newspapers in our house—a local Tamil newspaper and an English newspaper. My dad and I used to read both papers. While he was with his friends, someone brought the Tamil newspaper. My father was very excited and opened the paper to the third page to see the results. He told everyone that my name would be featured in the first-class column. So, he looked at all the numbers in that column—to his great surprise, my number was not there. He was disappointed but did not give up hope. Then, he looked at the second column, where the second-class candidates' numbers were given. To his great surprise, my number was not there either. He was even more disappointed as he looked at the third column with the third class results. My registration number was missing there as well. He thought I had done well, he had had a lot of confidence in me, but he was seeing something else. He began to walk home slowly. In the meantime, at home, we received the Tamil newspaper first and my brother anxiously opened the paper. We did the same thing as my dad—we looked at the first-class column, then second-class column and, finally, third class column. My number was not to be seen. I told my brothers that it could not be true. I had done very well in all subjects except one. Everyone at home was very sad and gloomy.

Within half an hour, the English newspaper arrived. I decided to check the paper by myself, so I opened it and looked at the column for first class. To my surprise, my number was there! I could not believe it, so I shouted to my brothers, —Oh my brothers, look at me! I got the highest grade!" I had passed with a high honor degree. My brothers were very excited. Unfortunately, we could not yet tell our dad because there was no phone. So we waited for him. Dad came home, feeling sad, thinking that I did not do well. As soon as he came, I shouted that I had done really well—I had achieved the highest honor in my class. He was so relieved! I can still see his face; he was so happy. That day, we had a special lunch prepared by mom. We all sat together, talked, laughed and ate. My Amman, my Shakti, performed a miracle that day. She helped me believe that whatever the situation, whatever may have happened, She would always be with me and I would be fine. From that day forth, I always heard her voice in my inner being, and I never gave up hope, no matter what happened. Later on, I found out through my school that I had stood first in my class in the final. My hard work had paid off. I kept my dream alive—I owe that to my second brother, who was wise and affectionate. He passed away recently and I still miss him. Brother, I will always love you and remember you.

The good news about my accomplishment spread quickly among our relatives. My dad was very excited. He told me that I should apply to medical school as soon as I received the application forms. In those days, in our state, there were only five state-owned medical schools and one private-owned medical school. There was also one federal government-owned medical school. The state school usually took two hundred students in each medical school—so, about 1,000 students were admitted every year. The federal government-owned school took in only fifty students from different parts of the country. At that time, there were only five federally owned medical schools in all of India, and getting admission into any one of them was regarded as being very prestigious. Since I got excellent grades, my father felt that I should apply to both schools; I might get selected to the prestigious one. I did not have the courage to tell dad that I preferred to go to the state school than the federal school; at his urging, I applied to both schools. Since I was only 16 years old, I did not want to go far away for schooling. The federal school was almost 300 miles away from my home but one of the state schools was only about 150 miles from home. Also, I knew that my Birth Mate, whom I had met at pre-university, had applied only to the state school and was hoping to be accepted.

The time came for my interviews for the state and federal schools but they were held on different dates. I was accompanied by dad for the state school interview. Three people interviewed me; they had my grades in front of them and asked me why I preferred medicine and what was my purpose for entering the profession. Since I was only 16, and had no fear, I answered them courageously. I believed that fear is the absence of faith—so long as I have faith in my Amman, my Shakti, I would be fine. I felt that I did very well in the interview for the state medical school. The results were to be published after a few days in the newspaper. Two days later, I went for the interview with the federal school. I knew that they only selected 50 students, and a lot of students had turned up for the interview. Initially, I was a bit scared on seeing such a big crowd. The interview went on for the whole day and included a physical exam. To my surprise, at the end of the day, they told me I had been selected. So, even before I knew if I was selected for the state school, I had received admission to the federally owned school. This was quite an honor, as not many people received the opportunity to get into the prestigious school. My father was very excited and paid my tuition fees right away. On the way back home, on the train, my mind was going on a different route. I decided that, if I were to be accepted by the state school, I would rather go there since it was closer to home and there was a chance that my Birth Mate would be accepted there as well. I did not tell my father about my preference because I knew it would make him unhappy. After a few days, the state school results were published in the paper. As expected, I was selected. I soon found out that my Birth Mate was also selected. Then, I told dad that I would rather go to the state school. My father was very upset since getting admission to the federally owned school was very hard and was regarded as a great honor. Also, the money we had paid for admission would not be refunded. He told me, ―If you make a decision, you must take the responsibility." So, here again, I was a little rebellious but the decision I made this time had a lot of positive effect in my later life. I told dad, ―I will go by myself to the federally owned school and get all my papers back."

I wondered about how my destiny had changed again. When I was in the ninth grade, I made the decision to go into medicine, against my dad's wish. That changed my destiny and I had begun dreaming from those days of becoming a wonderful doctor. Then, my destiny changed again when I finished high school and, against my dad's wishes, my second brother got me into a wonderful Catholic college. Now, I had chosen to go to the state-owned medical school rather than the prestigious federal medical school. Here again, my dad showed his greatness by accepting my decision. I wondered where my destiny would lead me now.

Chapter Six

THE ART OF HEALING: THE NOBLE PROFESSION OF ALL TIME

What is success? Is it wealth, is it power, is it honor, is it knowledge?

Success is a state of mind.

—Unknown

Coming back to the morning of July 5th, the second day after I was admitted to Rush Medical Center. I was sitting in my chair. My mind was clear even though my right arm and right hand, as well as my right leg, were still weak. My coordination and balance were off. I had a real problem even with brushing my teeth, because my right hand was not cooperating. Even if I wanted to stand, I needed help. I was in a state where I needed help constantly but still felt that I was going to recover completely. Because of my willpower and my Amman's power, as well as the wishes of all my loved ones, I knew that my recovery would be successful.

The first medical person I saw that morning was the physician in charge of physical therapy. He was a young guy, and he greeted me with a pleasant smile and asked me the routine questions: How I was feeling, asking me to raise both upper arms and then my leg, and asking me to stand up if I could. We had a nice chat. He told me that I would have my first physical therapy session soon, probably that afternoon. After that, I saw the speech therapist, who seemed to be a wonderful person. She asked me my name, age and date of birth, where I was now and what the time was. These were all questions everybody had asked me for the last three days, so I was ready with an answer as soon as they were asked. She also told me I should start trying to write. She then showed me some pictures and asked me to identify them—all basic things that kindergarten kids have to learn. I did not feel bad because I knew that I had to start from scratch; I really felt it was a good start. After that, the neurologist made his first round. As I have said earlier, he was the department chief at Rush Medical Center. There was a huge crowd behind him and, when he entered the room, some residents and students followed him in. He asked me the routine questions, and he was very kind. He examined me, and reassured me that I was going to be fine. After that, a young lady came and introduced herself as the cardiologist and did her routine exam as well. She said she was going to order some more tests, which included Doppler studies on my lower legs and an MRI of my heart. Then she left. Now, I was a little exhausted. By the time my breakfast arrived, I was having a real problem trying to eat by using my hand. My wife helped me—and I really appreciated that nice gesture.

As I lay in bed, awaiting my daughter's visit, my mind went back to the day I entered medical school. I was very excited. Even though I was a teenager, I was mentally mature and ready to face the challenge. My dad took me to the medical school. There, I made two friends—one of whom was my Birth Mate. The other one, whom I just met, also came from the same district as my Birth Mate and myself. The three of us instantly became great friends, just like the three amigos, and had a lot of fun during our college days. Unfortunately, the new friend, a very loving and affectionate person, later became addicted to alcohol. He passed away a few years back. I still think about him.

Finally, the dream of going to medical school had come true—thanks to my strong faith and hard work. We had 200 students in my class—127 boys and 73 girls. Among the male students, I was a little shorter and slimmer. My height did not bother me at any time in my life. At several points, and during my early school days, many people had talked about my height—especially some of my relatives. My father was above average height but my mother was short; I knew that I carried my mother's gene and it did not bother me at all. Not once did I think that height was a factor in obtaining my goals and dreams of becoming a fine doctor. I had strong faith in myself and my Shakti.

In the first few days of school, I met three more, very important, people—all of whom changed my life positively. One of them, who came from a town in my district, was very smart, pleasant and well organized.

He was focused on his education. From now on, I will refer to him as our Think Tank. Then, I met another interesting classmate who was my next-door neighbor in the dorm. He was five years older than me—compared to most of the other students, who were my age. I considered him as my older brother. He gave us good guidance and leadership, which we all benefited from later in our life. From now on, I will refer to him as our Leader. He liked me and I liked him too. That friendship was cemented for a long time but, unfortunately, he passed away sometime back. Our Leader's roommate, who was also in my class, became a good friend of mine. He came from an average family but was very bright. He studied well and, even used to teach us how to prepare for exams. Even today, I have a good relationship with him.

When I was in higher secondary or high school, we had only boys attending the school; I never went to a co-education school. Even after I finished high school, when I entered the one-year pre-university, it was in an all-male Catholic school. So, this was the first time in my life that I experienced co-education. This was a great source of excitement for us as we were still teenagers. I was 16 going on 17, and we were all terribly excited to see the girls. Every one of us had a crush on some girl. In the early days of medical school days, I had a crush on one of my classmates. She was a Christian and a very nice girl. That crush died out within a year and I had a crush on another Christian girl—that crush lasted for a couple of years but, finally, it also passed on. These were all one-sided crushes, as we did not have the nerve to go and talk to the girls or express our desires and feelings. Later on, I found out that if you liked somebody, you should always find a way to talk to that person. If it works out well, it is okay; if it does not work out well, that is okay, too. The reason I had reservations about these girls was that they came from different religions. In those days, most marriages were arranged by parents or families, and love marriages were not encouraged. Because of my respect for my family's tradition, I did not want to hurt them. In fact, some years after we finished medical school and everybody had entered into their different life paths, I met both of my _crushes' at different times; both of them were very nice to me and they are wonderful people. I cherish their relationships. They are married, have children and grandchildren and are doing very well in life.

At that time, medical school was for five-and-a-half years. In the first year, we focused on English, chemistry and biology. For the next one-and-a-half years, we had anatomy, physiology and biochemistry; during the next three years, we studied pharmacology, forensic medicine, ophthalmology, pathology, surgery, medicine and gynecology and obstetrics. At the end of each section, we had written and oral exams, as well as a lab exam that was called a practical exam. We had to pass both the written and oral exams together, and the lab exams separately. So, if someone did not pass the lab exams even though they did well on the written and oral exams, they were still failed. In fact, while we had two hundred students in the first year, only 30 people passed through the final year without any problems and entered the training program, which was called house residency. The rest followed, after passing their exams. Luckily, with belief in myself and faith in my Shakti, my Birth Mate, Leader and Think Tank and I sailed through the five-and-a-half years with flying colors. This was our _Gang of Four'.

During my second year, we had to dissect a cadaver in anatomy class. It was a good experience. The exercise did not bother me as we did it as a group, and were all learning together about the human body. I was an easygoing, happy student. The good days lasted until my third year of medical school. I was just 21 years old when my life slowly moved in a downward direction. The year before, my dad had been losing weight but did not tell anybody. I later learned from my family that he had had some trouble sleeping at night. I knew that my dad was a smoker but, at that time, no one told us that smoking could cause serious lung problems. When my second brother came home for vacation, he noticed that dad had lost weight. When he commented about the weight loss, my dad did not admit to it. However, finally, my dad admitted that he was losing weight, did not feel like eating and, sometimes, had a really hard time sleeping. So, my brother brought my dad to my medical school, and we consulted a surgeon. That was the first mistake I made—I was just a medical student and I thought a surgeon could perform miracles. My first thought was that dad possibly had cancer of the stomach. A routine chest x-ray was done and they found some fluid in the lining membrane of the lung called the pleura. At that time, tuberculosis was prevalent so the surgeon diagnosed my dad as having tuberculosis with pleurisy. Without doing proper tests, he told my dad to go back home and take medicines for tuberculosis, which included daily injections and oral medications. So, my dad came home and, faithfully for three months, took the oral medications and the streptomycin injections that in and of itself were very toxic. There was no improvement. By the time I went home, I saw there was no improvement in his health; he was going downhill. So, we took him to another doctor who performed a pleural aspiration and found a lot of blood in the pleura. That is what we call a hemorrhagic pleural effusion in medical terms and, from that, the doctor thought my dad may have had cancer of the lung—which was the cause of his problem. At that time, we were ignorant of the fact that my dad has cancer because of his smoking habit. We accepted the fact that my dad had cancer of the lung and he was taken to a very good hospital far away from our hometown, where he stayed for three months. First, we thought he was going to have surgery to remove the cancerous tumor from his lung but when they did what we call a bronchoscopy, they felt the tumor was too far advanced to be removed surgically, so he was given chemotherapy and then sent home. So, my dad was home and was seen by a local doctor for continued treatment.

I knew that my dad was gravely ill, and that I may lose him in the near future—that thought was foremost in my mind while I was in my third year of medical school. One day, when I was preparing for an exam for ophthalmology, I received a telegram from my oldest brother saying, _Dad is in serious condition, please come home'. As soon as I read it, my inner instinct felt that something was terribly wrong. I did not know what to do. I showed the telegram to my friend, our Leader, and I told him that I felt my dad had passed away. He consoled me and said, ─Don't worry. Go home and do what you can but come back immediately since we just have one more week to prepare before the exam. After the exam, you can go home and go through your grieving." For some unknown reason, I felt brave and said, ─Okay." So, he sent me home by bus. By the time I reached home, there was a huge crowd at my home, so I knew that something bad had happened. I went inside and I saw the body of my dad lying there surrounded by my family. That same evening, we took our dad to our village, where he was buried. In our culture, we did not keep the body of a deceased person for more than 24 hours, as we did not have mortuaries or the equipment to keep a dead body in a frozen state. At that time, my third brother who was far away in medical school in his final year, and was preparing for his final exam within a month, arrived very late. Luckily, he reached our village at the time of the burial. That day was very painful but I remembered my friend's words: ─Please come and finish your *karma*, your duty." That is what my Dad always used to say, too. He gave much importance to education and always told us to do well in school. This was evidenced by the fact that, even when my dad knew his death was imminent, he would not allow my oldest brother to inform my other brother and me of his condition because it would disturb us when we were preparing for our exams. My two brothers, my mother and three sisters were at his side at the time of his death. He was a wonderful human being and a loving dad who really cared about our well-being. At the time of his passing, my youngest sister was just 11, my next sister was 13 and my oldest sister had just turned 19. My older brother was the only one who was married at the time of my father's death. At the time of dad's death, my mom was only 53 years old and my dad was only 59.

A memory from the time I was in ninth grade surfaced. I had told my dad that I was going to medical school. One day, after my father and I went to the Nagaraja Temple for our early morning worship, he took me to one of his friends, who was a palm reader, to read my future. The friend was not a professional, so he did not charge for the reading. He was just a very close friend of my dad's and was a school teacher who had the gift of reading the future. My dad told him, "I want my son to be with me always, even at my old age. So, tell me what you think." My father had told me that, after I finished medical school, I should come back and start a clinic in our town to help poor people—that was his dream. My dad's friend read my palm and said, "You know what, this guy will go far away from you. Even you cannot see him. He will be far away—that is his destiny." I looked at that man and said to myself, —What is he talking about?" but that prophecy was lodged in my brain from that day on. After my dad died, a lot of things changed in my life. I don't know if it was my destiny or my dream or my Amman's plan.

Now, I have to say a few more things about the last days of my dad's life. He was at home, and I think he knew that he was going to die because his body was slowly giving way. Day by day, he felt weaker, he was not able to even stand up, and he lost a tremendous amount of weight. However, he was very conscious, very alert and never ever complained to my mother about any suffering. He never said that he was going through a very painful situation. When people came to see him, he always told them, —I am going to be fine at the end." The day before he passed away, he spent the night with his favorite nephew—his oldest sister's eldest son. Both of them really liked each other, and the nephew was almost like my dad's son. My dad had lost his sister when she delivered a baby, and died of postpartum hemorrhage—so, my dad was especially loving towards their family, and his nephew was very special to him. In later years, this nephew became a *sannyasi* (similar to a monk)—in our religion, this is a renunciation of material wealth and family ties. He was a very wealthy man, he was married and had children but, one day, felt the calling to become a *sannyasi*. Since then, he lived a very simple life. On the day of my father's death, they spent the whole night praying and singing God's songs. In the early morning, my dad's nephew told him he was going to be fine and then left our home. Then, close to nine in the morning, my dad was completely alert and calm and knew what was going on. He called my brothers to him. My mother was there but did not know what was going on. She was a very nice person but innocent. My dad told my two brothers, —Now you have to take care of the family. Everybody should be okay." Then, he looked at my mother calmly and asked for a small cup of water. He quietly drank the water and passed away. It was a very peaceful death with no struggle—that was what I was told. I am not surprised about his final passage from this earth because he was mentally very strong, deeply religious and spiritual, and very kind. He knew that it was his time to leave and he went with dignity.

It is interesting to know that November 22, 1967, the day my dad died, was the fourth anniversary of the assassination of the American President, John F. Kennedy.

During my college days, my friends and I had a lot of fun. I was a casual smoker at that time (not a regular smoker) and did not know that smoking causes lung cancer and other lung-related diseases. How ignorant I was, even though I was in medical school. Even after my dad's death, I continued to smoke, though not on a regular basis.

When I was in medical school, I met another interesting person who became my friend; he was my Birth Mate's roommate. This guy was very smart and liked to play the guitar during social hours; he introduced me to music. At that time, ‚Beatlemania' was going on all over the world, after the Beatles successfully toured the United States. So, through my friend, we learned about and liked all the Beatles' songs, especially Paul McCartney and John Lennon's songs, which were very popular during our medical school years. This friend always dreamed about going to Los Angeles and New York, saying this was the new world where he wanted to go. At that time, I had no interest in such places and neither did my Birth Mate. We made fun of him but every time we talked to him, he would somehow or the other talk about America, the big cities there, and so on. So, at that time, there was some idea in my mind that there was something far away we could explore in the future. Unfortunately, the guy who always talked about going to America was unable to go to the United States. He is still living in India and is very successful. However, for some reason, he was not able to even visit America.

My Birth Mate also loved music and played the *bulbul tarang* that he had brought along with him. He was very talented and gifted in terms of music. I called him a musical genius. At the end of our second year at medical school, we had a school function in which I wanted him to play the *bulbul tarang* but he was hesitant and shy. So, one night, I took him to the top floor (roof) of our college and he spent the whole night practicing his music. Finally, he felt good and said that he would play for the function. So, the college function came and he played—and everybody appreciated him and loved his music. Within a year, he ran in the college election for finance secretary and won with a big majority. After that, he bought a guitar and, with another friend, played it at college functions. He has explored music in great depth throughout his life.

I believe that I played the role of a catalyst. Do you know what a catalyst is? It is a person or thing that precipitates an event but does not get any credit for it. Yet, it always enjoys the good things that happen. Throughout my life, I have played the role of a catalyst.

Before I finish this chapter, I have to share two interesting experiences. One was a big surprise, and the other a near-death experience. The first experience happened when we finished our final exams in the final year of medical school. Usually, once the exam was over we all knew unofficially whether we got through or not, and whether we could go onto our one-year internship before we would become a doctor. The official results would be published in the paper a few weeks later. If you did not pass all the subjects, you would have to wait for six months to retake the exam. I thought I had done very well. So, once the exams were over, I asked my roommate to go and check whether I had passed all the exams. When he came back, he didn't look happy, so I asked him, ─What is going on? Are you okay? Did I pass?" He said, ─No, you failed in one subject." I asked, ─Which subject?" He replied, ─Surgery." I could not believe it. That was the subject in which I thought I had done exceptionally well. Anyway, the rest of the Gang of Four all passed the exam. So, I accepted my fate that I would have to wait the six months and then catch up.

One other guy from our batch, who was also a good friend of mine, had also failed in that subject. This friend and I went to the movie theater and watched two shows continuously through the night and came back in the early morning. Everybody then left for home. I went home and told my brothers, ─I am sorry, brothers. I failed in one subject, so I have to wait." In the meantime, my third older brother had passed his medical school and was undergoing his residency program. So, during that vacation time, I was enjoying my time off. The day of the official results announcement came. The English newspaper was delivered, and my brother asked me, ─Hey, do you want to check your results?" I declined but he asked for my registration number so that he could check. To my surprise, my number was there! I had passed all the exams! Not only had I but the friend who thought he had failed had also passed the exam. The biggest moment of joy was when my friend, our Leader of our Gang of Four, whom I considered my brother, looked at the results, found my number and immediately telegraphed me saying, _You have passed'. That was the greatest surprise and enjoyment. The only thing I missed in all this was my dad's presence. Remember the time I faced a similar situation in my pre-university final exam results, where everybody thought I had failed, but I actually scored first in my class? Once we found out the pre-university results, we all sat together and had a nice lunch. This time, we dined together again but without dad. Finally, after a couple of weeks, I came back to school, and we started our house residency.

Next, I want to talk about my second near-death experience. I had mentioned in a previous chapter about how, in my early years, I nearly drowned in my village river but was saved. This time, I was in the second or third year of medical school when our Leader invited us and a few other friends to go for a picnic near his hometown. His place had beautiful small hills, and the place we went to had a beautiful waterfall. We were able to swim at the base of the waterfall. Even though I did not know how to swim, I went into the water. Our Leader was sitting on a rock and watching us. A few of us were playing in the water. The water was not very deep so I was a little bit brave; slowly, I went closer to the waterfall. Unfortunately, there was a lot of wet sand beneath; all of a sudden, my leg went down and I was unable to come up. *Oh my god! I am drowning*, I thought and felt that I was going to die. I was unable to shout but I waved my hands. Some of the others thought I was playing a game but one guy—thank god—saved my life. I am always thankful to him. He saw that I was struggling, so he immediately grabbed my hand out and I escaped death this time, too. I know my Amman is always with me and that I still have some more years to live and do good things. That day, we had a good time at the waterfall. Later, my friend arranged for dinner, and we were served some local liquor. At that time, there was strict prohibition in our state and liquor was not allowed. I used to drink occasionally but not regularly. That evening though, because of the stress of my near-death experience, I drank heavily and almost collapsed. I did not know what had happened until the next morning when my friends told me that I drank too much. In the next chapter, I will tell about our experiences during our house residencies (internship) and our future plans.

Chapter Seven

DREAMING TO COME TO THE NEW WORLD, THE WONDERLAND

When you have made up your mind what you want to do, say to yourself a thousand times a day that you will do it. The best way will open soon. You have the opportunity you deserve.

—Unknown

Affirmation is with God. All things are possible and that keeps reminding us that possibilities existed though not yet here and challenges as to discern and realize those possibilities with God's guidance.

—Unknown

Coming back to the afternoon of July 5th—my second day of stay at Rush Medical Center: I was trying to remember the Sanskrit prayers I used to say every morning and before I went to sleep. To my surprise, I was able to remember all the prayers, which was evidence that my memory was still very much intact. Then, the physical therapist came and took me to the physical therapy department for the first time, where he gave me some coordination tests. I did very poorly because I had lost strength in my right hand, and I had poor coordination of my fingers—even lifting a pencil was very hard for me. However, I did not give up hope. I knew that with strong determination and deep faith in my Amman and in myself, I would recover from the stroke completely. So, I was very patient. Next, he took me for a walk but because of my right leg weakness I was off balance. He put a little belt around my waist and was holding the back of it, allowing me to walk. As soon as I developed a little confidence, he allowed me to walk by myself for a bit but stood behind me to make sure I did not fall. Then, he told me to walk up the staircase slowly; I was feeling a little more confident even though I was a little shaky. I felt this was a big accomplishment and was very happy. Then, I went back to my room and sat in my chair.

My daughter, who had flown in from San Francisco the previous night with her husband and two young children, paid me a visit. On seeing me in this situation, she became very emotional and was in tears. She and I always had very good conversations. I was very happy to see her and the time I spent with her and her family was quite uplifting. We had a fun time and she was happy to see that I was doing better, yet she knew that it would take me a long time to recover. Unfortunately, I was unable to see my grandchildren due to the hospital rules, which stated that children under 12 were not allowed. Both my grandchildren are very young, and my son-in-law was taking care of them while my daughter was visiting me. My daughter said that my son-in-law would come and see me later.

After my daughter left, another friend of mine from medical school, who used to be the roommate of our Leader, came to see me. He was the one who used to help us study to get through the exams. He is now living in Chicago and doing very well in his practice. After he left, my Birth Mate, who also lives in Chicago, came to see me—which was a good surprise. He was attending a conference in another state but, as soon as he heard the news that I was ill, he immediately flew back to Chicago and came to see me. It was a good feeling that my family and friends cared so much about me, and that I was surrounded by a lot of loving people.

I was very exhausted that evening. While in bed, my mind raced back to the days when I had finished medical school and started my one-year house residency. We had to rotate every three months in different departments, such as surgery, medicine, OB-GYN and social medicine. After we finished this rotation, we would receive our diploma and could start practicing as a doctor.

After we all finished medical school, we left for our homes to spend time with our families before starting our residency. Some changes had taken place in my family after my dad's passing. My elder brother was currently taking care of our family. The relationships between his family and my mother and the rest of my family members were not as cordial as before.

Finally, we all came back after our brief vacation to start our one-year residency. Our Gang of Four was back together. From then on, most of our important decisions were made as a team.

My residency was basically uneventful but there were a few things that happened in my life. I used to inform the Gang of Four of everything that was going on and they also did the same. However, there was one thing that I did not share with them. This was about a resident whom I knew was involved with drugs. At the time, there was a drug called pethidine (Demerol) that was given to patients after surgery as a pain reliever. It was a very common drug used for post-operative patients at that time. This resident was using that drug as an injection, and I also tried it with him on a few occasions. I did not share this with my close Gang of Four. Later on, after using this drug a few times, I figured out that was not the best direction for my life; I kicked the habit on my own. Because of my strong willpower, which I developed from a young age, I went cold turkey. From then on, I have not used any illegal drugs, or any drugs without a prescription from a doctor. Later on, I heard that my friend had died of a drug overdose. What a waste of a great mind! I was, however, still smoking at that time, but did not realize that smoking causes lung cancer—which was the cause of my dad's death. I will tell you later about how I stopped that evil habit completely.

The residency program was the time when students usually made plans for their future. Most of my classmates in the training program wanted to join government-owned hospitals. At that time, India had social medicine, just like in the British system. There were very few self-owned private hospitals but most rural hospitals were managed by state governments. Each year, they recruited doctors who had just graduated from the current program. So, there were plenty of jobs at that time. The salary for a doctor was very high compared to the other professions—800 rupees. One American dollar was about 8 rupees then, so the earning was about a hundred dollars. However, that was more than enough for a single person. Most of my classmates applied for the government jobs, but we—members of the Gang of Four—as well as another friend decided to do one more year of the residency program, called senior residency. In the medical system, after finishing a second-year house residency, you were eligible to enter postgraduate specialties, which included surgery, OB-GYN, pediatrics, medicine, and so on, or enter government service, work for a while and then apply for postgraduate studies. We preferred not to enter government service and do just the second-year residency. It was a very bold decision because, at that time, none of our families were very rich. Everyone had problems at home and our families expected us to get a job. In any event, we all applied to the second-year program; however, our Think Tank also applied for and got a government job but because of my persuasion he dropped that offer. Thankfully, he listened to me—I will tell you how it changed our lives at a later point.

We decided to do our second-year house residency at the prestigious central institute called Jawaharlal Institute of Postgraduate Medical Education & Research or JIPMER in Pondicherry, which is near Chennai. That was the place my father had initially preferred me to go to for medical school. I had been accepted and we had paid my tuition but I had declined it against his wishes. All of us who applied (Gang of Four and one more friend) were accepted.

During our residency program, our thoughts were going beyond what we should do. Our Think Tank informed us that we should think about going to the United States. He said that there was an exam called the Entrance Commission for Foreign Medical Graduates (ECFMG), which we would have to take if we were to be accepted for a residency program in the United States. The exams were in English because they wanted to test how fluent we were with our English, and our medical subjects. This exam was a bit different from the ones we had previously gone through. We had a British system, with essay-type writing but this system was multiple choice—and we had never sat for such an exam before. I will tell you later how it affected me for the first time.

My friend gathered all the information about how to apply for the exam. Unfortunately, there was no place in India where that the exam was offered—it was offered only in Sri Lanka and Malaysia. Since we all knew that we were going to do one more year of residency program at JIPMER, we knew that we had to take the exam during that second year of our house residency program. Even though our Leader was not fully convinced about going to the United States, he said that if we wanted to apply, he was okay with that and we would all apply. So, at the end of the first year of house residency, we got the forms, filled them out and applied together—all except for my Birth Mate. I will tell you why later.

Once our Gang of Four came back from the short vacation, we arrived at JIPMER for our second-year house residency program. The ECFMG exams were conducted only twice a year—one exam in the early part of spring, and one in the later part of fall. Since we had just joined the senior residency, we applied for the second session. All of us (Gang of Four and one more friend), except my Birth Mate, applied for that year, and planned to go to Sri Lanka to write the exam. The other friend had relatives in Sri Lanka at that time; when we were there, his relatives took good care of us.

While at JIPMER, I developed a special interest in child care and elected to do my second half on child care in the pediatric unit. In the earlier period of our training, through our Think Tank, I was introduced to a very interesting guy who came from a different medical school; later, he joined our group. We were all wondering who this new guy was—our Think Tank was always talking about what a smart cookie he was. He talked about his work ethics, and how he was always on time for work. I was a bit jealous after hearing all these things, so I was not impressed when I met him for the first time. I thought he was a nerd. However, the more I got to know him, the more I knew I had been wrong, and the more I liked him (along with the rest of the Gang of Four). Later on, he became not only my mentor but changed my life for the better as well. He and his future wife (whom I met after I arrived in the United States) taught me the true value of compassion, empathy, kindness and love, and the true meaning of friendship. From here on, I will refer to this person as my Mentor.

During my residency at JIPMER in 1970, I had six friends including the Gang of Four, the other friend from my medical school and my Mentor. My Mentor, who applied for the ECFMG exam in Sri Lanka (during the spring session), successfully passed on his first attempt. The format of the exam was multiple choice, which we had never experienced. While I was doing the second half of my pediatric training, the assistant professor, who really liked me, gave me a book to prepare for the ECFMG exam (he had already taken the exam and passed it). I did my best to read it, even though I was on call every other day during our residency and was having a tough time. In the fall of the same year, the Gang of Four, except for my Birth Mate, along with our other friend from my medical school, took the exam in Sri Lanka. This was my first experience of flying, and the first time flying out of my country. The trip was less than an hour from the town where the airport was but it was a pleasant experience for all of us. The exam, as I remember, was held over one day with a morning and evening session. There was one part that was for English proficiency. I thought I did fairly well but I did not know exactly how the outcome would be. During our stay in Sri Lanka, our friend's relatives treated us very well. We stayed with them and they took us on a tour around Sri Lanka for one week. It was a wonderful experience.

My Birth Mate did not apply for the ECFMG exam that year, as he was planning to marry his sweetheart, who was from his hometown, in the summer of that year. He opted to take the exam the next year, and successfully passed it on the first attempt.

Finally, the results came—to my surprise, I did not pass the exam. For the first time in my life, I did not pass an exam on the first attempt. The friend who had arranged our trip also did not pass the exam. Remember, we were the two guys who were told in the final year exam in medical school that we had failed in one subject but later found out that we passed. That time, we were lucky; this time, out of the four of us, only two passed. Luckily, there were three chances to take the ECFMG exam—but if we did not pass within the third attempt, we could not ever try again. I took this very positively. I am always a dreamer and I have strong faith in myself and my Amman. I knew I could take the exam at a later date. My initial plans for going to the United States with my friends were dashed but my Leader, Think Tank and Mentor, who all had passed the ECFMG exam on their first attempt, applied for residencies in the United States for the following year.

This made me think that I could do a two-year fellowship, with one year in child healthcare, as I was finishing up my two-year house residency. In 1971, I applied for that fellowship and was accepted at my old medical school. My friend, who had failed that first attempt at the ECFMG exam, applied for fellowship in surgery. While my other friends were preparing to go to the United States for their residency programs the following year, I was preparing to join my old medical school for a fellowship program in pediatrics.

Two members of our Gang of Four (my Leader and Think Tank) and my Mentor were accepted for residency programs in Chicago, and landed there in the summer of 1971. After our second year of residency, my Birth Mate (who married his sweetheart in the summer of 1970), joined JIPMER as a staff member in 1971. That year, he too passed his ECFMG exam on the first attempt and, in 1972 (after being accepted for residency), came to the United States with his family. My Mentor got married in the summer of 1971 before they left for the United States but his wife stayed in India in order to finish her schooling and joined him a year after. I attended their marriage in their hometown.

I was a little disappointed at leaving my friends for the first time after such a long time together. I returned to my old medical school and completed the one-year pediatric fellowship called Diploma in Child Health (DCH) and passed my exam with distinction. I came first among my fellow residents with flying colors.

I smoked throughout medical school and residency programs. My dad had been a smoker and had died of lung cancer. Even so, I did not know that smoking caused lung cancer. How ignorant we all were then— and some, even now!

After I finished my DCH in the spring of 1972, I returned to my home for a brief period before I joined as a pediatrician in a local Christian missionary hospital in a small town near my hometown. My home situation was not cordial. The relationship between my mother and my elder brother had deteriorated. We had a joint family system and my elder brother, with his family, took care of the rest of us after our father's death. In the meantime, my second brother got married and was living in the same house. We lived in a two-storied house. My mother, two of my unmarried sisters, and my second brother and his wife were living on the first floor for a brief period of time. My eldest brother and his family lived on the second floor. My eldest sister had already married in 1971, while I was doing my fellowship in pediatrics. There was a lot of misunderstanding between the family members and I felt the heat. In the late fall of 1972, my third brother (the doctor) married and began to live on his own.

In the summer of 1972, I started working at a Christian missionary hospital in my local district as a pediatrician. At that time, there was no pediatric unit in the hospital—in fact, there was no pediatrician. I was the first pediatrician in that hospital to establish a pediatric unit. I worked as much as I could. Because this was a missionary hospital, I took care of very poor and sick children. Infant mortality was very high, even though I did my best to save as many children as I could. Some days, I felt terrible at losing a child despite my best efforts. During my stay in that hospital as a pediatrician in the fall of 1972, I took the ECFMG exam in Malaysia since there was no center in Sri Lanka at that time. I had a very good name in the missionary hospital. I was well liked and the superintendent of the hospital wanted me to stay. However, I had a different plan. My dream was to do a residency in the United States in pediatrics, and pass the pediatric board exam. Also, I wanted to join my Gang of Four, who were already in the United States.

My friend, who did not pass the exam the first time, went with me. We stayed in Singapore for a few days with my friend's relatives, and we had a good time. This time, I got good news—I passed the exam with flying colors! My friend also passed the exam. Our plan was to travel together to the United States in the summer of the following year. When we left India, my friend was already married and had a daughter, who was a year old. When we landed in London on the way to New York, on July 17, 1973, we celebrated his daughter's first birthday there. I still remember that sweet memory.

At this point, I have to mention one of my medical school friends, whom I have referred to as one of the three amigos. I loved him dearly. He was not in my original Gang of Four but was still very close to me at that time. I had a wide circle of medical school friends, and he was a part of that circle. When I decided to take the ECFMG exam in Malaysia, I asked my elder brother to help me with two-thirds of the cost. I did not feel it was right to ask for all of it, as I knew my family was going through a difficult time after my father's death. As a doctor, I was making only 600 rupees a month. I borrowed the remainder from my friend, who borrowed it from his brother-in-law; I paid him back before I went to the United States. When I needed to buy three suits before leaving India, I again borrowed 1,000 rupees from him. That was a great help and I repaid the money in full after I arrived in the United States and started working as a resident. Unfortunately, this friend later became an alcoholic and passed away very recently. That was a big loss for me.

My home situation was getting worse day by day, so I decided that I had to make a tough decision before I left India. The relationship between my mother and elder brother was not positive, and my mother was not happy about the home situation. We worked out a compromise—my eldest brother and his family could inherit his portion from my father's wealth and leave our house permanently. Also, my second brother would take over caring for my mother and two unmarried two sisters and manage the rest of our family's funds. While I was a pediatrician in the mission hospital in 1972, my third brother got married; before that, in 1971, my eldest sister had gotten married. When I left India, neither my two younger sisters nor I were married.

Because of the sad situation in our family, I was not in a good state of mind when I left for the United States.

I need to mention a very important turning point in my life before I finish this chapter. I used to smoke throughout medical school, and even while I was a pediatrician in the mission hospital. Before I left for America, my mother looked at me one day and said, ―Son, you are going to go far away from me, I can't see you or talk to you. You know that your dad died of lung cancer...Why don't you stop smoking?" Remember, I told you my mother was very smart, and her instinct was that smoking was not good for anyone. At that time, I did not feel that I should stop, but her words struck me like a bolt of lightning. I didn't say anything. A few days before I left for the United States, I went to a movie. When I came out, I bought a pack of cigarettes from a store and was about to start smoking when my mother's words came to mind. At that moment, I knew exactly what she meant. I threw the cigarettes away immediately—to this day, I have not touched a cigarette. I developed strong willpower from a young age—once I decide I should to do something, I am able to do that. I am really thankful for my mother's golden words and my willpower. Since I decided to quit smoking, I decided to stay away from alcohol, too.

I have always believed that our mind is as a servant and we are the master. As long as you use your mind as a servant, you can make sure that the mind does a good job. But, if the mind takes over and acts like a master, you lose the game. I knew that I was the master and I had to make sure that the mind was filled with positive thoughts. Luckily, because of my deep faith in my Shakti (Amman), I rid myself of both evil habits.

Chapter Eight

COMING TO AMERICA, MY DREAM COME TRUE

Our beliefs about ourselves are the most telling factors
in determining our level of success and happiness in
life. When the voice and the vision on the inside
become more profoundly clear and louder than the
opinions on the outside, you have mastered your life.

—John F. Demartini

Going back to my recovery—on the morning of July 6, 2016, I was sitting in the chair. The nurses came and checked my vital signs. The neurologist came and examined me; he felt that I was doing much better and told me that I would be discharged by the next day. He also told me that I should continue the occupational, physical and speech therapies at home, and see my neurologist once I was released. I felt much better at that time. The cardiologist came and ordered a bunch of tests—an MRA of the heart and Doppler leg studies. Then the physical therapist came and I had one more session. It was very encouraging. I was able to walk a little bit better and felt more confident. During the MRA, I had to go through the procedure under a tunnel—it was a little scary but I chanted some *mantras* and closed my eyes throughout the procedure; I was able to do better then. The Doppler studies seemed to be much easier. After I came back from my tests, my daughter and then my son-in-law came and spoke to me. My son and his best friend, the neurologist, also visited me. Everyone encouraged me saying that I would do better but I knew that everything is within me. Once I believe that I will do better, I know that I am going to get better. So, I was not going to give up. I felt a bit tired, so I lay down on my bed and my thoughts went back to my past.

I finally landed in the United States. I had finished my two-year house residency and one year fellowship in pediatrics, as well as a one-year stint as a pediatrician at a Christian missionary hospital in India. At that time, the Indian government allowed only eight dollars to be carried as foreign exchange. The value of one American dollar was about eight rupees—so, after spending sixty-four rupees, I had to travel with eight dollars on hand. Luckily, the place where I was accepted for my residency paid my airfare with the agreement that I would pay it back when I started working at the hospital (with paycheck deductions). I knew this was a good idea since I did not have enough money to buy the airfare myself. I felt very good. When I arrived in America in July 1973, I was 26 years old— a young, unmarried man. Even before I left for the United States, our Leader (who at that time was doing his second-year residency in Brooklyn, New York) had sent a money order for one hundred dollars for my friend and me—we were both very grateful for his generosity. We both felt very good that we had enough money. Now, whenever I meet up with my old friends, we still talk about the foreign exchange we received and jokingly refer to ourselves as _eight-dollar people'.

It is interesting to note that when I came to the United States, I was on a J1 visa for my residency in pediatrics, but as soon as I landed in New York, I applied for a green card to stay in the USA. After five years with the green card, I was eligible to apply for naturalized United States citizenship.

The night before I left for the United States, I spent one night with my sister and her family. She prepared a wonderful meal and I still remember her kind gesture. She was a very loving, wonderful soul. She is no longer with us; she died of breast cancer a few years ago. I still remember her unconditional love and I am very thankful for having such a loving sister.

I have been a self-motivated, goal-oriented person throughout my life from a young age, and did not know the true meaning of love. I have had good experiences throughout my life with people who really cared about me, but only three people have really taught me the meaning of true unconditional love. Three people have changed my life forever. My sister, who passed away, was one among those three. For that, I am eternally grateful to her. I will tell you later about the other two people from whom I learned the true meaning of love.

My friend, with his young family, and I landed in New York on a bright day on July 17, 1973. We were a little tired but very excited. At the airport, the Leader of our Gang of Four greeted us with a big smile. He was accompanied by my Mentor's wife, who also greeted us. From the first time I met her, I could see the sisterly love and affection—she was one of the three people who taught me about the true meaning of selfless love with no expectation. I am very grateful for her kindness and compassion. Thank you, sister.

From now on, I will call our group as the Gang of Five, that includes my original three friends, and the friend I met at JIPMER and refer to as my Mentor. The Gang of Five was as follows: the first was the Leader, the second was Think Tank, the third was my Birth Mate, and the fourth was my Mentor. All of us were in the United States. The Leader was doing his second-year residency in Brooklyn, New York; Think Tank was doing his residency in Chicago, Illinois, and my Birth Mate was doing his residency in Flint, Michigan. My Mentor was doing his residency in the Bronx VA Hospital in New York. I was doing a residency in Bronx, New York, in a very nice hospital. The friend who accompanied me with his family was doing his residency in Manhattan, New York. We had all arrived at different times—Leader, Think Tank and Mentor in 1971, my Birth Mate in 1972, and I in 1973.

I found a place to live in the basement of a rental house, with another person who was three years junior to me in my medical school. I did not know him but got to know him after I landed in New York and we became roommates for the first year. I spent the first half of that year in Fordham Hospital. It was a couple of miles away from my residence, so I took the subway to reach my work most of the time (since I did not have a car). In the latter part of the six months, I worked in Misericordia Hospital in East Bronx. This was just a few blocks from my apartment, so I used to walk to work. At that time, in 1973, there were no Indian shops or restaurants, and there were very few Indians that I saw when I was walking on the road. To get Indian groceries, we had to go a Jewish shop in midtown Manhattan. So, whenever we wanted to get something, I had a friend who would give me a free ride in his car. I really enjoyed those outings.

I had been accepted in my residency as a straight pediatric intern without having to go through rotating internship. I had been given a one-year exception because of my previous training in India as a pediatric fellow. So, I was happy that I could finish the pediatric residency within three years. Whenever I had free time, I would spend much of it with my Leader and Mentor. On some weekends, my Mentor's wife cooked delicious vegetarian Indian food and we all enjoyed it. By observing their sincere love and compassion towards others, I developed a very close relationship with them. His wife's love reminded me so much of my sisters back home, and I considered her one of my younger sisters. She is the second person through whom I learned the true meaning of love. My Mentor was also very kind to me, and I felt in my heart that we had a close spiritual relationship—much like brothers.

During the first few days of my residency, I felt very lonely and cried a lot. I overcame that feeling soon. Then, one evening, when I was on call at Fordham Hospital, I looked out of the window from my room and saw some fine white flakes falling from heaven. I thought this was a wonderful experience that was happening to me! I didn't know what it was but I was very excited. I called my friend and he said this was the first snowfall of the season. Since I had not seen snow before, I got very excited and started singing. Seeing snow for the first time was a very joyful, spiritual experience.

As far as food was concerned, I was not a vegetarian. When I was young, my mother used to cook fish for four days, and vegetarian food for three days of the week. Due to some religious reason, which she never explained to us, we had only vegetarian food on Sundays, Tuesdays and Fridays. Since we came from a tropical place and lived close to the sea, we usually had plenty of fresh sea fish. Sometimes, my mother used to cook goat meat and chicken but we never ate beef or pork. So, when I came to the United States, I was a little hesitant to eat hamburgers but, out of necessity, I began to eat it on some occasions. Most of the time, I lived on salad, eggs and bread. During my first year of residency, the hospital provided free breakfast and lunch. So, most of the time, I ate there; at night, I ate other food.

My roommate was a strict vegetarian. He loved to cook but I did not want to, since I had not learned how to cook. So we made a deal—he would cook and I would wash the dishes. That really worked out well.

In those days, not only were there no Indian restaurants or Indian shops, there was no place where we could go for worship. However, they had started building a Ganesha temple in Queens, New York, in 1970. In the latter part of my residency, I used to go there often. Later on, multiple Indian stores popped up in the Queens area—to my surprise, those areas became bigger and bigger. Lately, when I visited New York, I could not believe how the Queens area had changed since I lived there some 40 years back. Some things were not even recognizable.

In the latter part of that year, I felt that I should have a car because asking friends to take me to places was becoming difficult. My Leader suggested that I buy the Super Beetle—a very popular, small car made in Germany. I thought, *What the heck! I will get a new car*. Therefore, I bought a four-cylinder, fully air-conditioned Super Beetle in blue (my favorite color). It cost only about four thousand dollars at that time. The fact was, I did not learn driving properly before I came to New York. I took two or three lessons in India and got an international license. With that international license, I was able to drive in America but I did not know the local traffic laws or the proper way of driving. So, after I got the car, I took some private driving lessons; however, as I was only making nine thousand dollars per year, I felt these lessons were very expensive. Even though I was a bachelor, I was sending money home and all my expenses were eating away my salary. So, after two days of lessons, I decided not to take any more lessons and started driving my car. The first two days were hell! I was driving in a crazy manner but finally learned the art of driving. Later on, I became a master in driving throughout New York even though I never had a map to follow. At that time, there was no navigation system in the car. Fortunately, I never had an accident while I was in New York for three years—that is a miracle! God is great! The first trip we made with the Super Beetle was with my Leader, Mentor and his wife. We drove all the way to New Hampshire. We went to see the White Mountain and had a very nice time. This was a wonderful time spent with all of my friends. I became even closer to my Leader even though I had already considered him my best friend and my brother. Now, I truly experienced his true love towards me. He is the third person in my life through whom I learned unconditional love. Also, I felt that my Mentor and his wife had become a part of my family; even today, I feel the strength of that relationship.

The year 1973 saw a lot of turmoil in America's political system. At that time, Nixon was the President (he had been reelected in 1972), and the Watergate scandal was going on. I liked politics from a young age. As I told you, my dad was involved in politics at one time and then he quit. Being a social reformer, he cultivated the love of politics in me. So, as soon as I landed in the United States, I read and listened to political development and the drama of Watergate. In 1974, I saw Nixon's final speech before he resigned his presidency. It was a poignant moment in my life in the United States.

Whenever I drove, my favorite recording artist at that time was Barry Manilow. For some reason, I enjoyed his voice and listening to his songs.

After I finished my first year of straight pediatric internship in the summer of 1974, I wanted to go for my second-year residency in pediatrics at the same hospital but the hospital only offered me first-year residency, as there was no position available for the second year. I did not want to do that because I had already had my straight pediatric training there. My Leader, who was then finishing his second-year residency at Maimonides Medical Center in Brooklyn recommended my name to his Chief of Pediatrics and secured a position for my second-year residency in that hospital. The sad news was that, by the time I was ready to go, he had decided to move back to Chicago, Illinois, and start his neonatology fellowship at Cook County Hospital, which was a two-year program. My Mentor also decided to move to Chicago to do one more year of chief residency at St. Francis Hospital in Chicago. It was a shock for me because I had assumed that they would be with me. Now, I was going to miss these three wonderful people very much. I realized though that I would still be able to remain in touch with them. I also have to share a sad event that happened during my first year in New York. One of the medical graduates from our medical school, whom I had known before (from India), committed suicide. That was my first experience in the United States of seeing somebody who was really jovial and wanted to do well in his life end his life suddenly.

In 1974, I started my second year of residency in Brooklyn. It was a very good hospital. The hospital had their own apartments for medical residents. I wanted to get one of those apartments because it was very close to the hospital. I would be able to walk back and forth to the hospital even at night. However, there was a rule stating that they would only give those apartments to a married resident. At that time, I was not married but I always wore a ring that was given to me by mother, bearing my name. So, my friend suggested, ―Why don't you just tell them that you are a married person?" and when asked just pretend that your ring was from your wedding. I do not like to lie because it is not a good feeling. Out of necessity, however, I told them that I was a married guy and they gave me a one-bedroom apartment. It was a very nice apartment, so I was happy with that. The rest of the people who were staying there were all married. Each time I went to the hospital, my co-residents would ask me, ―When is your wife coming?" I always told them that she was still in India and waiting for the visa. I told them that as soon as she gets a visa, she would come and join me. Everybody respected me as a married man, and that was the safest thing that happened during my second year in residency.

Making phone calls to our homes in India was very difficult and expensive, so we always communicated with letters. It would take approximately a week to 10 days for the letter to reach our home. By the time I got a reply from my family, another 10 to 15 days would pass by. There was no cell phone, text messages or Internet, so it was very hard to reach people who were living abroad. Through letters, I knew that our family was doing fairly well.

Coming back to my second-year residency, I had a wonderful experience in the hospital. I worked very hard. I missed my three good friends—my Leader, Mentor and his wife, who were in Chicago—but I kept in touch with them through phone calls. The Think Tank was still in Chicago, doing his residency and my Birth Mate was still in Flint, Michigan, doing his residency. We always kept in touch via phone and our relationship is still very strong.

Before finishing my second-year residency in New York in 1975, I made a trip to Miami—driving all the way from New York via Washington D.C. and back. I was joined by a friend, his wife and their two wonderful children. This friend and his family had arrived in New York in 1974 for his first-year residency. So, I told him that I would be the driver and we could go and see some places. It was an inexpensive but wonderful trip. We covered almost 3,000 miles. That was the best journey I ever had.

Another time, I also visited Niagara Falls, with a good friend of mine from Chicago and his mother. This friend and I always had candid conversations about the existence of the Creator. We always agreed to disagree. I valued his love and friendship. His mother was a very intelligent lady, despite having had no early education. If she had been well educated, she would have been our first woman president!

During my second-year residency, I wrote the first part of the board exam for the American Academy of Pediatrics in New York and passed successfully. However, I would have to wait for two years for the oral exam before becoming board certified in pediatrics, and travel to San Francisco for that as well. I will tell you more about my San Francisco trip later.

Among the Gang of Five, only two were married at this point—my Birth Mate (who was now in Flint, Michigan) and my Mentor, who was in Chicago. In 1975, my Leader went back to India and got married. I was unable to attend his marriage because I was doing my residency at that time and was also in the midst of getting my green card. So, sadly, I missed his marriage. I consoled myself with the fact that I would see my Leader and his wife when they returned to the United States.

At the end of my second-year residency in the summer of 1975, I applied, and was accepted, for a fellowship in newborn medicine (neonatology) at a hospital in Newark, New Jersey. At that time, it was called Martland Medical Center but now it is University of Medicine and Dentistry of New Jersey. There, I met one of my senior college mates from my medical school, whom I did not know very well while I was in India; now, I got to know him better. In the summer of 1975, while I was doing my third-year residency in New Jersey, I took my license exam in Washington D.C. and passed it. This would allow me to practice medicine in the United States.

When I joined my third-year residency in neonatology, my Leader was still in senior residency in neonatology in Chicago and my Mentor returned back to New York to do a two-year fellowship in hematology. So, I was really excited to see him and his wife, and they were both very excited to be back in New York. Most of the weekends, when I was free, I drove all the way from New Jersey, crossing the Long Island Bridge, to meet them. They lived at that time on Coney Island in New York because he was working at the Coney Island Hospital. That year was a wonderful time. We used to go to the Ganesha Temple on weekends. Some Indian stores and restaurants had popped up. We liked to eat the Indian food there sometimes but, more often, my Mentor's wife cooked us fine delicious vegetarian food. I used to stay with them for much of the weekend. I will never forget those days. The bond between my Mentor, his wife and myself grew stronger and stronger. Our relationship is still very strong. Those feelings are still within me and I value this wonderful relationship.

In the meantime, I wanted to go back to India to see my mother and siblings. It has been almost three years since I had visited home. I was told that I would get my green card before the end of my third-year residency (before the summer of 1976).

I started thinking about future plans. The hospital I was working in had only a one-year program for neonatology. So, I had two options. I could either go into a second year of the neonatology program on the West Coast or in the Chicago area, or I could start my private practice in any part of the United States. My goal was to go to the West Coast. At that time, most of the residents I knew from New York went to the West Coast after finishing their residencies, and most of them were located in the Los Angeles area. So, I really wanted to go and settle there—that was my dream. However, I believe in destiny. One day the Leader called from Chicago and asked, "What is your plan?" I told him I wanted to go to the West Coast. He said, "Listen, you come to Chicago and we can set up your practice in the Midwest." I asked, "What practice?" He replied, "I am going to finish my second year in neonatology fellowship, so either we can start a practice in Chicago or some other place." At that time, I had no idea of what I should do, so I said, "Let me think about it. I will let you know."

In the meantime, my green card was granted and my residency came to an end. I told my Leader, ⎯Let me go home first and see my mother and the rest of my family. When I come back, I will decide about my future plan." He agreed. I told my Mentor and his wife about the conversation I had with my Leader, and also that I had not decided my future plans. In the meantime, the Think Tank was still in Chicago; he was planning to do a further fellowship in adult gastroenterology. He wanted to go back to India to get married. I felt that, since I was going back to India, I should get married, too. Our custom at that time was to have our marriage arranged by the family. Each family talks to other families, and then if they like the family and if the boy and girl like each other, they get married. I felt it would be much easier if my brothers could arrange a marriage for me.

When I went home in the summer of 1976, my second and third brothers were both married; my eldest brother had already left our home and had his own family. I told my mother and two brothers that I would like to see my eldest brother. So, my sister's husband and I went to see my eldest brother and his family. He was nice to us. Even though he did not maintain eye contact, he listened to me and things worked out in an amicable manner.

Coming back to my marriage, it was proving to be a bit tough because, at that time, Indian families were very conservative and sending their daughters to America was a scary thought. No one wanted to marry their daughters to a guy who just landed up from America and said he wanted to get married. I was a little disappointed. A couple of weeks before I was to return to America, my brother said there was a very good family he knew. A cousin's sister had gotten married to their family; they said they would approach the father of the girl and talk to him about me. To their surprise, they were willing to listen to my brother's proposal. So, that was how I met my future wife. She was just finishing her college. We met each other and the family decided we should get married. I wanted to get married right away, while I was still there, but my wife's family felt that they could not arrange for a wedding so soon. It would take a couple of months' preparation so they asked me to go back to the United States and come back in the early part of the following year. So, our marriage was fixed for early February 1977. I was a little disappointed but said that it was fine.

After spending a few days in India, I returned to New York. I met my Mentor and his wife at the airport. We drove back and I stayed at their home because I had vacated all my things from New Jersey. Then, I decided to go to Chicago to see my Leader. So, I packed everything I owned in my Super Beetle (there were only a few things). I drove all the way, crisscrossing the country from New York to Chicago via Detroit. I visited my Birth Mate and his wife, and I spent a day with them before leaving for Chicago. When I reached Chicago, I stayed with my Leader, who was just married (in 1975), and stayed with him and his wife for a few days. Then, we started to look for a practice. He had finished his residency and was doing some moonlighting to pay the bills and feed his family. I stayed with him. One day, one of his friends suggested that there was a good opportunity in a rural town in West Central Illinois looking for pediatricians. My friend said, ―Why don't we go and look at that place?" So, we drove to that rural town, it was about 170 miles from Chicago. As soon as we saw the town, we liked it. We met the hospital CEO and the doctor, who was to be our future employer. We liked the place so we decided to start our practice as partners in the wonderful town called Galesburg, Illinois.

Chapter Nine

THE ART OF HEALING; DANCING WITH GOD'S ANGELS, THE INNOCENT CHILDREN

When you have made up your mind what you want to do, say to yourself a thousand times a day that you will do it. The best way will soon open. You have the opportunity you deserve.

—Unknown

On July 6, 2016, I was lying in my bed and getting some rest. That afternoon, two of my colleagues from my hometown came to see me. During our conversation, I told them I would be discharged the following evening and that I would like to be home by July 8th. One of my friends offered to drive my wife and me back when we were ready to go home. It was a very nice gesture, and I really appreciated his compassion. However, not knowing what my plans were to be, I told him that I would let him know after discussing it with my wife and my son.

After my dinner, I was resting. My mind went back to the time we started our practice as pediatricians. Before I went to the Midwest, I always felt that I did not want to go to a place that was very cold. I always wanted to go to a warm place—and had decided that I would settle down on the West Coast. But my good friend, our Leader in our Gang of Five, wanted me to go to the Midwest and start a practice with him. Because of his unconditional love, and since I knew that he cared for me, I reluctantly said, "Okay, I will come." I thought it was a good idea to have a partner because from the beginning; I did not want to start establishing a practice on my own because of the expenses and call schedule.

I have to tell you something about the town we selected to settle down for our future practice. At that time, it was a booming Midwestern town in Illinois, and the population was close to 38,000. A new mall had opened just the year before and, wherever you went, there were a lot of young people. It was a factory town—there was a refrigerator factory belonging to the world's leading producer for refrigerators, as well as a lawnmower factory and a couple of other small factories. The town was booming. It was very impressive in the late 1970s. After we talked to the hospital administrator and the doctor who sponsored us (who was an obstetrician) for our practice, we got two apartments—one for me, and one for my friend and his wife. It was a beautiful apartment complex and our apartments were a couple of blocks away from each other. The real estate guy who got us our apartments was very nice and kind. Later, we found out that he had had some business dealings with the doctor who sponsored our practice. I often went to my friend's apartment after work and enjoyed the good dinners prepared by his wonderful wife.

Initially, we had been promised that we would be paid 30,000 dollars per person per year for a one-year contract—that was good money and I was very excited. Also, knowing that I would be going back to India within a couple of months to get married, I was living in a dream world and was extremely happy.

We opened our office on August 19, 1976. The first office we had was behind a McDonald's fast food restaurant. It was a nice office. Later on, I found out that the rent was paid by the hospital but that the owner of that office was our employer. In the later part of that year, 1976, my life was pretty easy. The practice was not very busy but I did not mind it. In my high school days, I used to write poems in Tamil, my mother tongue. I did not continue that practice while I was in medical school but now, all of a sudden, I had the urge to write some poems. I was thinking about my beautiful future wife and I wrote a couple of wonderful poems in Tamil.

In the local community, there were a few more Indian doctors, and most of them were married. Most of them were working with a clinic, and the friend who brought us to this small town was also working in our hospital. Later, he and his wife also became close friends of mine.

I had a lot of free time in the latter months of 1976. On November 17, 1976, I wrote eight Commandments', just like the 10 Commandments in *Ben-Hur*. They were:

Pray to God every day.

Whatever you do, do it perfectly.

Do not think of harming anybody.

Stay consistent with your principles.

Get rid of laziness.

Talk carefully and cleverly.

Control your emotions.

Realize the truth and then talk.

I kept those commandments in my original handwriting in my office—and have been following them until now. My friend wanted to exercise, so he asked me to run with him in the early morning. I never ran in the morning—I used to walk when I was in medical school or ride a bicycle. Because of his persistent requests, I started running in the early mornings with him. Also, our other friend joined us. The habit of going for a run in the morning helped me during the latter part of my life, and I am very thankful to my friend for initiating that good practice.

In the meantime, my friend's wife was pregnant (she was pregnant when we came to Galesburg). She delivered a wonderful boy in the third week of November. It was a joyful occasion at that time. Our other friend's wife was also pregnant at the same time and she had had a baby the month before. Both babies were wonderful boys, and I really loved those children.

The winter of 1976-77 was very severe. In those days, the Midwest winters were very bad, with a lot of snow. I had never experienced this type of winter while I was living in New York—it was that severe. I knew that I was going to leave for India in early 1977 and was happy as I would be back in warm weather. I was also euphoric thinking about my marriage. In the third week of January 1977, I left for India. The one thing I did before I left—which was a stupid thing—was to shut down all the pipes in my apartment. I thought I was saving energy, but did not know that the severe winter cold can damage the pipes. I found out only after I came back that my whole apartment had been flooded and that they had had to call the plumber and electrician to take care of the damage. The insurance covered the cost of the damages, and, luckily, they did not make me pay for this mistake, but I was embarrassed and ashamed.

In December 1976, my middle sister had gotten married. After my marriage, I had only one sister who was waiting to get married. Most of my family was settling down. I got married on February 2, 1977. My wife's father was like a godfather to the whole family. He was a self-made businessman, and a very kind and hard-working person. My wife was his only daughter; she had three brothers. Every member of my wife's family took part in the marriage, and the wedding was held in their home. We were married in the early morning. To my happiness, my Birth Mate and the Think Tank attended my wedding. My Birth Mate came with his wife and two young children. The Think Tank got married within ten days after my wedding, and I attended it with my wife. It was a very happy occasion. All members of our Gang of Five were now married, and we were very happy with married life.

After I got married, I went back alone to the United States because my wife had to wait to get her green card, which would take about two months. Upon my return to Illinois, I heard through my friend and other people that the second half of February of 1977 had seen the coldest weather in the history of our town— most of the time, it was sub-zero temperatures. Luckily, I had escaped that weather; by the time I returned, it was cold but not severe.

Before I go further, I have to tell you about something that happened two months before my marriage. Luckily, with the grace of my Amman—my power—I escaped death. This is the third time I escaped (I had almost accidentally drowned twice before). This happened during the winter of 1976. While preparing to go back to India, I had ordered a tailor-made suit in Chicago. When the suit was ready, I went back to Chicago. At that time, there were few Indian tailors who provided custom-made suits. Since I am short, I couldn't get proper suits in department stores.

It was a very cold winter day and it was forecast that we might have snow or even freezing rain that night. I had never driven before in freezing rain, as New York weather was very different, and I was ignorant about driving conditions in the Midwest. Anyway, I picked up my suit and then met two friends of mine for dinner, before driving back to Galesburg. When I said I was going back to Galesburg after dinner, they did not want me to drive because of the bad weather forecast. They said, ―Today is not a good day to drive. Why don't you stay overnight and go in the morning?" I declined because I had to be at work the next morning. I was afraid that due to getting up in the morning and driving all the way, I might not reach work on time. So, going against their advice—because of my total ignorance and idiocy—I drove home in my Super Beetle. In fact, I was driving a little fast. Within an hour after I left Chicago, I was stopped by a policeman and given a warning. He said, ―Listen, you are driving a little too fast—go slow." Thank god he didn't give me a ticket! I continued my journey. I was about 14 miles from Galesburg and it was past midnight. I was half asleep and there was a truck in front of me. I was driving behind him and, foolishly, trying to overtake him. I don't remember what happened after but, by the time I woke up, I was in the ditch. Luckily, I was unhurt. I wore a seatbelt all the time. The car was completely damaged. When I got up and looked around, a policeman was there. He helped me to get out of my car; to my surprise, my suit was intact. I had had it made for my wedding day and, it was called a _marriage suit'. So, luckily, I survived another near-death experience. Then my Leader, whom I now call my partner, came to my rescue. It was almost early morning. It was very slippery on the road, so he drove very slowly and took me home. That was one of the worst experiences ever but also my good fortune. That was one of the coldest winters in our town's history. We faced similar weather during the month of February.

In the meantime, I was preparing for the second half of my board exam for pediatrics. I had to go to San Francisco in April 1977 to appear in person in front of three examiners. It was an oral exam as well as a clinical exam. I was very confident that I would be able to pass both exams. My wife was planning to come to the United States in April, as she had received her green card; she was to travel with one of my friend's wife. My plan was to appear for the exam, and then fly from San Francisco to New York to receive my wife. One of our senior classmates from our medical school was in Los Angeles at that time. His wife was also appearing for the second half of the board. He helped me by accompanying me to San Francisco since his wife and I were taking the exam at the same time. I did very well on the exam. In fact, one of the examiners was born in my town where I was now practicing, so he was very happy to see me and was talking about the greatness of our town. Then, I flew to New York and met my wife at the airport. At that time, my Mentor and his wife were still in New York, because he was finishing his fellowship. We stayed in their house and had a nice dinner the night my wife arrived. Then we flew back to our town. This was the first time my wife had flown from her hometown to a different place—in fact, a different country. It was a very strange experience for her but she was happy that she was with me.

Life was going smoothly at that time. I was not very responsible since my Leader, my partner, was with me and the practice was going okay. Every two weeks, I got a paycheck. I didn't have much responsibility but the cloud was approaching slowly and steadily—I would learn about this later. It would shake me up a bit but because of my faith in myself, and the power of my Shakti within me, I was able to work through all heartaches.

In the summer of 1977, I did not think my Leader/partner was completely happy, even though he had just had a baby. Also, we found out that my wife was pregnant with our first child, and was due to deliver in the early February 1978. One day, my partner gave me some unexpected news—it was a shock for me. He told me that he was planning to move to Texas to set up a new neonatology unit at a hospital where he had been offered a job. Initially, I did not want to believe it. He said I would be okay and this practice only needed one pediatrician. I did not like the idea because, from the beginning, I had never wanted to go on my own. I always wanted to be with somebody as a partner for a couple of reasons. One, it gave me some time off and the calls were shared. Two, the responsibility was shared; I did not want to take complete responsibility. However, I was pushed to a corner and there was no other way I could say _no'. Having married recently, and with a baby on the way, hearing this news made me very nervous; I was angry and upset with my Leader. However, I also felt that the time had come for me take full responsibility. My Leader told me that he would be leaving in the fall of 1977 to start his new practice in Texas. I realized that this was the end of our first-year contract.

So, my employer gave me two options: The first was I could continue to work under him with the same status quo. The second option was I could go on my own. The problem was that, if I wanted to go on my own, I needed money to set up a practice. I had very little by way of funds. There was some money in the outstanding patient charges (collection) but sometimes it takes several months to collect this so I did not know what to do at that time. I was a little confused.

A few days before my Leader/partner left town, he had a one-on-one conversation with me. That was the first time I expressed all my feelings openly—in fact, it was kind of a heated outburst, but he was very gentle and never said anything. He just listened. I vented all my anger and frustration about him leaving me and pouring cold water on me but he did not say anything. I know that he was aware that I was hurt, so he did not want to hurt me anymore. The night before my Leader/partner and his wife left our town, I requested them to stay in our house but he preferred to stay at another friend's house. Then he left. I felt sad but thought it was okay. After he left, I was left alone. I was still employed by our current employer but I was seriously thinking about doing something different. I was still practicing in the same building, which the employer owned, and we had one office secretary who was appointed by him. In the meantime, our hospital was building a new building for physicians. I went and asked the hospital administrator for an office space to practice in the new building, as I was planning to go on my own. He promised that they would have a pediatric floor for me on the third floor. Once I had that promise, I approached my employer and told him that I had decided to go on my own. He was a good businessman and he told me that it was okay if I wanted go on my own, but there was still money in the collection that was not yet collected. So, he told me that I could have that account and start my practice but I would have to pay a certain amount of money before I become self-employed. At first, I thought it was a good idea—then again, I would have to borrow from the bank since I did not have that much money. I did not think the bank would give me a loan because I did not have any equity. So, instead, I wondered about going on my own, starting from zero and letting my employer be responsible for the money the practiced owned—the money still there on that account. I told him, "You know what, I don't want to take any of that money. You can have all that collection and I will start from scratch." He was a genuinely nice person and said that was fine, but I would need some money anyway to start my practice. I would have to pay the rent, and electricity and phone bills, and hire a secretary. At that time, the person who had been working with me was leaving the practice to become a teacher. She told me that she knew a girl who was young and smart—she would ask her to come and meet me. If I liked her, that girl could be my new secretary. I had no previous business experience or knowledge of how to manage my own practice. So, there was a lot of responsibility thrust on me all of a sudden. I went through a lot of stress that I did not tell my young wife about, because I did not want her to worry while she was pregnant. The only thing that helped me throughout my career was my early morning jogging—a habit of being an early riser that I had developed from my school days. I was usually up at four a.m.; I would go for a run (around three miles), come back, take a shower and then go to work. I continued this practice for seventeen years until my left knee began to hurt. I stopped running but continued to walk in the morning hours. The habit of running/walking helped me to feel better because of the natural increase in endorphin and dopamine levels in the brain. It really helped me to face the day-to-day challenges in my new practice with confidence.

In order to start my practice, I needed some money but I did not want to ask my friends or take a loan from the bank. I knew that no one would give me any money at that time. So, I decided to approach the CEO of the hospital and ask him for a loan. He seemed to be a nice guy—the first time we had visited Galesburg to meet him before we decided to settle down in this town, he was very cordial, encouraging and straightforward. So, I made an appointment with him and told him that I wanted to start a practice on my own. I told him I needed a loan. I told him that I could repay it within six months—a maximum of one year, but I was confident of repaying it in six months. He looked me straight in my eyes and asked me how much I needed. Before I went to meet him, I had no idea how much I was going to ask but I had a gut feeling to ask him for ten thousand dollars. So, I asked him for ten thousand dollars as a loan and promised to pay it back in six months. There was no written agreement—it was only a face-to-face conversation. Believing in me and my honesty, he said, —Okay, doctor, I am going to give you this money, and you will be fine." I was very happy and thankful. Even today, when I am thinking about those days, I thank God I survived because of all the wonderful people who helped me and believed in me. Thank you so much!

There was some more good news, too: I was told that I had successfully passed the second half of my board exam, so I was now a board-certified pediatrician. That was my dream come true; soon, I would become a Fellow in pediatrics. At the same time, the new construction for the hospital office building was started. I was told that we would be able to move to the new building in the summer of 1978. So, with that confidence, I told my employer that I was going to start my practice on my own, and I would set a date to begin. I also told him that I would be moving from the current location by the summer of 1978. He agreed to that, and assured me that he would recommend me as a pediatrician to his patients. In our town, there were already two Indian pediatricians working for a private clinic. In our community hospital, I was the only pediatrician. So, I knew that I would have to work seven days a week, 24 hours a day, on call. I wanted to be healthy and take care of my family, too. I had a lot of responsibilities but I gained strength from my immediate family and my early morning running.

The winter of 1977-78 arrived. It was the same kind of weather as the previous year—we had had plenty of snow in January 1978. My wife was almost full-term and we were expecting the baby by the second week of February of 1978. Since she was the only daughter in her family, we both felt that we should call her mother from India to stay with us during her delivery time. My mother-in-law accepted our invitation to come and stay with us for at least a month, and we were very happy. Unfortunately, she could not speak English and knew only Tamil. However, since she would be staying with us, we never thought that would pose a problem. Our apartment was very comfortable since It was a two-story apartment with one guest room. In the meantime, I was slowly building my practice, working very hard day and night. Another positive thing took place. Before my first office secretary left, she brought a wonderful new lady to our office. She was very young and, the first time I met her, she was very quiet and humble but impressive. I said to her that I would hire her as my first office secretary. She was a very honest person—dependable and trustworthy. Over my long career, she was not just my office secretary—she was my bookkeeper, billing person, and front desk receptionist who answered phone calls and made appointments. She was a jack-of-all-trades and performed all her tasks at work marvelously. I still respect her very much.

We were expecting the arrival of our new baby. At the same time, I keenly felt the absence of my good friend, the Leader of our Gang of Five and my previous partner. We talked to him by phone on and off and it seemed that he was happy and he said he was very busy setting up his new practice. It was around this time that I received the saddest news ever—which turned my life in a different direction.

February 1978 was very cold and we had snow most of the time. February 11th was a very cold day and we had almost six inches of snowfall in our town, with lots of snow around our apartment. That night, I invited my friend for dinner since his wife was out of town. My wife, with the help of my mother-in-law, prepared a fine dinner even though she was full-term pregnant. We chatted happily through dinner. My wife sliced some apples for dessert; we were about to eat them when, all of a sudden, I got a call from one of my friends in Chicago. He did not usually call me so I was surprised to hear from him. First, he spoke in a low tone about how we were doing and what was going on. Then he said that my beloved friend, my Leader, for whom I had so much respect and always looked at up to, had suddenly passed away. The news broke my heart. I was so shocked, I did not know what to do. I told my wife and my friend that I was going to go for his funeral. I booked a ticket and asked my friend to keep in touch with my wife since she was due to deliver at any time. That night was a miserable one. My mother-in-law understood how sad we were because she knew the family. I was all set to leave the next morning. However, at around five a.m., my wife woke up and realized her water had broken and her labor had started. Given this, I could not leave my wife and mother-in-law to go to see my deceased friend. Since I was still in great shock over losing my Leader, I immediately called my other friend and told him the situation. He was a very kind man. He said he would travel on my ticket and told me, ─You take care of your wife." I immediately agreed. Then I called the obstetrician (our former employer) and informed him about my wife's labor pains. He said to take her to the hospital and get her admitted. At that moment, I had no feeling of joy or sadness; I was just numb. Faith and destiny were playing a game. I always felt that life is the dance and we are the dancers.

After I heard the terrible news about the demise of my dear friend, I was feeling very unhappy. This was my second personal loss—after that of my dear dad during the earlier part of medical school. At that time, my dear friend/Leader had been with me and comforted me. Now, after his demise, I had no one to comfort me. The only thing I did was to keep running, and that was my only outlet for emotional sadness and stress. Without that, I would have been done for a long time ago.

On February 12, 1978, my wife was admitted to the hospital in the early morning. It was prolonged labor and my son was not born until eleven that night. It was a wonderful feeling to have somebody with whom I could share my love and joy; at the same time, I was feeling very sad about losing my best friend. So, losing my best friend and seeing my newborn child was a strange experience. I could not explain how I felt but that moment changed my life forever. As I mentioned before, my friend went for the funeral. Later on, my deceased friend's (my Leader) wife and her 15-month-old baby came to see us with her father, who had just come from India. We lived through the sad event together as a family. She moved back to India for a short while, and then came back to my town and stayed there for a few years. She later moved back to Chicago and finally settled down in New Jersey. She is an amazing person. She raised her child on her own with strong determination and a gentle smile. I was so proud to see her son growing up very well and becoming very responsible. He always has a gentle smile and showed everyone a lot of love—just like his dad. He went to Yale to get an MBA, and is now working in a well-respected Wall Street firm in New York. I am so very proud of him. He recently married as well.

In the spring of 1978, we moved to a new house. The person who built the house had stayed in it for six months before we moved in—so it was a brand new house. Our baby was about 3 months old. Winter was waning and spring was settling in. By summer, I had moved to the brand new medical office constructed by the hospital, and I was very happy about that. I had hired a nurse because my practice was growing. I was working very hard, day and night—attending a C-section at midnight, taking care of the emergency room when needed, and taking calls. All this work made me weak. Two or three years later, I fell very ill and was admitted to the hospital with acute infectious mononucleosis (glandular fever), and was kept in the hospital for a week and then at home for one more week. I realize now that was because of my stress.

In the summer of 1979, my wife's parents and brother visited us for a month and then returned to India. In the fall of 1979, my wife who was pregnant with our second child, took our son back to India for a short visit. Our second child, a baby girl, was born at the end of December in 1979.

As I said before, when I was in high school, I used to write poems in Tamil. After my dear friend passed away, I wrote a poem about him. I also wrote poems at the time of my son and daughter's births. I also wrote a poem when my friend/my Leader's son was born in November 1976.

As promised, I paid back the loan taken from the hospital at the beginning of my practice. I was very proud of myself for that. I stayed in the new building, which the hospital had built for physicians, for three years. I then moved across the street to another office and acquired 10 percent ownership of the building complex. The nurse who had worked with me was leaving, but introduced her sister to me before she left. Her sister began work with me as a nurse. She was a wonderful human being, very family oriented and honest. She and my secretary worked with me for a long part of my practice. I really respected her. In later years, I added a part-time employee since our practice was growing. This girl was also a wonderful human being, and I had a lot of respect for her. Before I retired, I had moved offices six times. The first time, I was on a busy street behind McDonald's; then I moved to the new building that was constructed by the hospital in 1978; then to another building across the street from the hospital (I moved three times within that building); finally, I moved to newly constructed building built by the hospital in 2002.

My practice was growing rapidly, and I was carrying more than what one member could afford to. By the time I was 20 years into my practice, I felt that I needed to make a professional change. During that period of my practice, the overhead expenses were about 33 percent. I was able to keep my practice at that level, and that made me proud of my medical management skills. In the early months of 1992, I told my coworkers that we needed to get a computer. Initially, the girls did not like the idea, and were very reluctant to go down this road. I persuaded them that we all should take a computer course before getting a computer. Eventually, we did get a computer and they slowly learned the art of using it—then, they loved it.

After 20 years of running my self-employed practice, I was mentally drained and physically a little tired since I was solely managing the medical as well as the business aspects of the practice. One day, I was talking to one of the hospital personnel and mentioned my frustrations to him. He said, —Why don't you sell your practice to the hospital? We will manage your business aspect, and you can just focus and fully concentrate on the physician side." In those days, hospitals were buying practices, too. It sounded like a good idea but, before I made that decision, I wanted to make sure the hospital was going to keep all of my staff. Also, I wanted to talk to my coworkers about the hospital proposal. So, after a discussion with my coworkers, I agreed to allow the hospital to take over the management of my practice. In January 1997, I became a partner of the hospital—from that moment on, I had no idea of what was going on at the front desk as far as management of the practice was concerned. I thoroughly focused on taking care of my patients. Our practice was growing even more, so they wanted to add one more person. For a brief period, the hospital hired a nurse practitioner but that did not work out well. Finally, in the summer of 2000, we had a pediatrician, who just finished his pediatric residency, join the practice. He was a wonderful asset—a good family oriented, kind person. I was happy that we had one more person join our practice. Also, as far as coverage, I now had somebody to cover on call with me. At this point, the hospital had built a brand new office building and they wanted us to move there. Before I moved to that building, we added one more nurse to our practice. She was a very helpful, conscientious, family oriented and caring person. She helped our practice in a tremendous way. In the spring of 2002, we moved to the new office space. At the same time, the hospital bought another practice (two more pediatricians) who shared our pediatric floor, and they were a very good asset to our growing practice. As you know, on September 11, 2001, the great tragedy happened in New York City. We moved a year after that in the spring of 2002. I told everybody that this was my final move and I was very happy about it.

In the meantime, I made some personal changes to my lifestyle. I wanted to be a vegetarian for a long time. A few years after my marriage, I became a vegetarian. My wife, not by her choice though, also became a vegetarian. Also, I had been a runner for over 17 years but after I developed some knee problems, I started walking in the early mornings. We also moved again in 1998 after we built a new house in our town.

By now, both my children were grown up and were in college. My son went to Oberlin College in Cleveland, Ohio, for undergraduate studies, and later to medical school at the University of Illinois in Peoria. My daughter went to Illinois Wesleyan University in Bloomington for undergraduate studies, and then to Sarah Lawrence College in Bronxville, New York, for postgraduate education in creative writing. In 2000, we made a trip as a family to north India to see the Taj Mahal. That was the greatest experience for all of us— seeing one of the Seven Wonders of the World. In 2002, my mother passed away on Thanksgiving Day at the ripe old age of 87 years. She had lived very well— in fact, she lived for more than 35 years after my dad passed away. She was healthy until she fell and broke her hip. Subsequently, she was admitted to the hospital for surgery and did not recover. I went to India to attend my mother's funeral and her final farewell. Now, both of my parents had passed away.

The once booming town that I had moved to from New York to start my practice was now going downhill. In 2004, one of our largest employers of the town announced that they were moving their factory to Mexico. Instantly, close to 2,500 people lost their jobs. It was a great shock to the community. At the same time, our hospital was also going through a very difficult financial situation and was about to declare bankruptcy. In fact, when I was managing my practice, my overhead expense was only about 33 percent during all 20 years of practice. As soon as the hospital bought my practice and took over the management, the overheads doubled. The hospital was bought out by a big for-profit hospital corporation. Our practice was flourishing. Another nurse was hired for my partner who was a little older but a wonderful person. After her retirement, another nurse was hired for my partner. She was a very good person—she was always smiling and kept our office in a very pleasant mood. In later years, another fine nurse joined the practice. She was a very hardworking, family oriented and good soul. In the meantime, a few more people were hired to assist us at the front desk. They were all wonderful human beings and a great asset to the practice.

Unfortunately, I was involved with three malpractice suits throughout my career. It was very unfortunate but none of them were due to my mistake. In the end, all was well.

On December 18, 2008, on what would have been my father's 100th birthday, my eldest brother passed away in India from a heart attack. I was unable to attend his funeral. Also, in that same year, I learned the sad news that my loving sister, the one who always taught me what love is, was diagnosed with breast cancer. On January 20, 2009, I visited my sister when she was undergoing treatment for her cancer in India. That was the day of President Obama's first inauguration. When I was with my sister, she did not look well but was smiling. I had a candid conversation with her. On March 13, 2009, my sister passed away— on the same day as my second brother's birthday. Now, this is the third person whom I loved very much, besides my father and my Leader. All of them had passed away. A month after her death, I suddenly became very depressed and, for two days, I stayed in my home and did nothing. I recovered soon after. I think I was undergoing a lot of stress, and the feelings about my sister's demise had overtaken me. Luckily, I came out of it and did well.

While my daughter was in New York for graduate studies, she met her life partner, who was from New Jersey. She got married in 2005 and moved to the West Coast. In 2012, my son got married. He was in New York after he finished medical school; he went to Columbia in New York to do his pediatric residencies, where he met his life partner. She was also from New Jersey. The strange fact was that, the year before I came to our town in Illinois, I had lived in New Jersey. Now, both my children's life partners were from New Jersey. Don't you think this is a strange coincidence?

I have to mention some sad news at this point. In our practice, we had had four pediatricians. In 2005, one week after my daughter's marriage, our senior partner passed away while he was jogging.

After that, a young, female pediatrician joined our practice, and she really helped our practice to flourish because of her dedication and her efficiency.

I was getting along very well with our colleagues and office coworkers, and life was going fairly well for three years, before I had my major illness. The hospital had introduced the system called Electronic Medical Records or EMR. This was a new concept, after Obamacare was introduced in 2010. Earlier, we used to write by hand about the diagnosis in the medical chart and give prescriptions on a prescription pad. Once they introduced EMR, everything had to go through the computer including the history, diagnosis, plan of treatment and prescription for drugs. I am not a computer guy. When I was born, there was no telephone or computer—they all came in the early 1990s. I knew some typing but I was not an expert, so it was a struggle for me. But I did not want to give up; I always wanted to do my best. The hospital administration gave us training and I tried to do my best to do well alongside my young co-physicians. I did well but I could not finish my work during office hours, so I usually took most of the work home. This caused more physical and mental strain. Even though I continued walking and was very careful about my diet and regular medical care, I was subconsciously stressing out more and more—which I did not realize until after I had my stroke.

In the late fall of 2013, my father-in-law (who had treated me like his son after my marriage to his daughter) had a stroke and eventually passed away in the spring of 2015, having never recovered from his stroke. I have fond memories of him as a father and miss him very much.

In December of 2015, I lost my second brother. He underwent heart surgery, and died of complications.

I had now lost my two older brothers and the oldest of my younger sisters. I had one brother left, who is four years older than me, and two younger sisters.

In the meantime, some good news came my way. My daughter had two young wonderful sons, so I became a grandpa. My son had two wonderful little girls. On the day my son had his second daughter—June 18, 2016—I was very excited. I was unable to go and see the child immediately but my wife and I decided that we would go to see the baby during the July 4th weekend. Now, you know my destiny. I finished my work on that Friday (July 1st), and left for Chicago on July 2nd by train. That night I slept well in my son's house, with no stress. When I woke up on July 3rd, something unimaginable happened—I suffered a stroke. That is my true story, but it is not the end.

Chapter Ten

THE MIRACULOUS ESCAPE FROM THE BRINK
OF DEATH; COMPLETE RECOVERY; FAITH,
FRIENDSHIP AND LOVE HEALS THE BODY AND
THE MIND

*When you are inspired by some great purpose, some
extraordinary project, all your thoughts break their
bonds. Your mind transcends limitations, your
consciousness expands in every direction and you find
yourself in a new great and wonderful world. Dormant
forces, faculties and talents become alive and you
discover yourself to be a greater person by far than you
ever dreamed yourself to be.*

—Patanjali Yoga, 200 years B.C.

Life is the dancer and you are the dance.

—Eckhart Tolle

*You are pure consciousness connected to the universal
consciousness; the infinite intelligence; you are the
power source connected to the cosmic power.*

—Unknown

Now, on the fourth day of my stay (July 7, 2016) at Rush Medical Center in Chicago, I was ready to be discharged. I felt a lot better physically and mentally. I had great faith in myself that I would recover completely in due course. Physically, I was still a bit tired. That day, my daughter and her family left for their home on the West Coast. The neurologist came in the morning and informed me that I could be discharged the same evening. I was advised to continue the occupational, physical and speech therapies once I was back home. My good friend, who is also my family physician, had already contacted the occupational and physical therapy departments in my hospital for my further treatment, which was to begin in the early part of the following week. My neurologist from my hometown was on vacation, so I had an appointment a week after my discharge to see him. I was very thankful to all my friends and my colleagues who helped me a lot during this very difficult situation.

That evening, my son came and took us to his home, where I rested well. The next day, a friend of mine, who is also a physician from my hometown and who happened to be in Chicago at that time with his wife, offered to take us back to our hometown. The interesting thing was that this friend had had a cerebral bleed three months prior to my stroke; by the grace of God, he has recovered very well. His wife drove us all the way from Chicago to our hometown; it was a wonderful evening and I was very grateful to them. As soon as we reached home, another friend of ours and his wife greeted us in front of our home with homemade food—which was a very nice gesture and greatly appreciated. That was a very thankful moment in our life.

At this moment, I have to mention our great Indian Galesburg community. When I moved to this town, there were a few Indian families living here. All of them were married; they worked in two different hospitals as physicians and all of them had young children. Our children became good friends as they grew up. Our Indian community members help each other when the need arises. We have our annual Diwali functions every year and enjoy mutual support and friendship.

Over the weekend, my wife's niece came from Texas with her mother, who had come for a visit from India. The day after I came home (Friday, July 8, 2016), while I was resting in bed, I was praying to my Amman, the power in me, when a poem formed in my mind. It was in my mother tongue; I decided that, when I woke up the next morning, I would write it down. So, when I got up on July 9th, I told my wife's niece about the poem in praise of my power inside, my Amman, and asked her if she would help me by writing what I composed, as I could not pick up a pen to write. She gracefully agreed and wrote the poem. I read the poem with her—that was one of the most enjoyable moments in my life because, just a week after my stroke, I could compose a poem. That was a wonderful experience—a miracle!

119

The following week, I started my occupational and physical therapies. My insurance permitted me to have thirty sessions, three days a week, and I felt very good. Most people say that, after a major medical illness, there is a tendency to get depressed and anxious. I was a little anxious about the insurance coverage and not being able to work but I was not depressed. In fact, I was happy that I was getting better—and that feeling made me strong. The physical therapist was a very nice, young girl, and she taught me the basic things of how I should balance and walk. It was very difficult initially but I said I could do it. With that confidence, in due time, I picked it up well. At the end of the month, I was discharged from physical therapy because of my good progress but was advised to continue the therapy on my own. I promised to follow her advice. My occupational therapy went on for three days a week for more than 4 months. My therapist was very encouraging and positive. On the first day, she told me to read a book titled *My Stroke of Insight: A Brain Scientist's Personal Journey* by Dr. Jill Bolte Taylor, a Harvard Research Scholar. I ordered the e-book on my iPad and read it—it gave me a lot of encouragement. It is about a Harvard brain scientist who, in her late 30s, suddenly suffered a severe cerebral hemorrhage. It was a very severe, disabling event but, with strong determination, she overcame her illness. The doctors told her that a lot of improvement can happen within six months but, after that, the recovery can be very slow. Sometimes, there may be no progress at all. However, Taylor believed in herself and continuously did all the therapies by herself. It took almost seven years but she completely recovered. That gave me a lot of encouragement. Medical doctors believe that once you have a stroke, your recovery will be much faster in the first three months, and kind of gradual the next three months. After that, it is kind of status quo. However, that is not true if you do your homework and therapy. It may take a year or two, or even more—in Dr. Jill Bolte Taylor's case, it took seven years for complete recovery.

I recently read a study done by Dr. Gary Steinberg, the chair of neurosurgery at Stanford. He did a one-time therapy, which involved surgeons drilling a hole into the stroke patient's skulls and injecting adult stem cells in several locations around the area damaged by the stroke. This procedure showed progressive improvement in these stroke patients in their recovery process. This implies that the affected neurons do not die immediately after the stroke but are still in the inflammatory state—so, injecting the adult stem cells into the brain will reactivate the neurons.

I also read a couple of other interesting books. One was *The Secret* by Rhonda Byrne, which gave me a lot of confidence and determination that I was going to be completely healed. I always believed that, as long as you believe that you are healed, your body heals very rapidly. That belief system set in from the day I started my therapy. One of *The Secret*'s teachings is: ―All you have to do is ask, believe you will receive the guidance you want and then stay alert to receive your answer.

The supreme power of the universe is with you every step you take and all you have to do is rely upon its power and ask." It is a very powerful statement but I sincerely believe in that. I will tell you at the end of my story how I recovered completely.

Another book I read was *When Breath Becomes Air*—a *New York Times* bestseller by the late Dr. Paul Kalanithi. He was a brain surgeon, and only 37 years old when he passed away. At the end of finishing his neurosurgery residency at Stanford University, he was diagnosed with Stage 4 lung cancer. During his treatment, he courageously finished his residency and wrote this book. Before the book was completed, he passed away but the story gave an insight to life.

Life is not permanent but you have to live each moment with happiness. Also, very importantly, live at the present moment. Do not worry about the past, and do not be anxious about the future. It is mindful living if you always live at the present moment and live each moment with happiness. That gave me a lot of inner confidence. I read a book by Thich Nhat Hanh, a Buddhist monk from Vietnam, who has written several books. I found his *Fear: Essential Wisdom for Getting Through the Storm* very interesting. In it, he quoted five remembrances, which made me feel a lot better. One, I have to grow old; I cannot escape growing old. Two, I will have ill health; I cannot escape having ill health. Three, I will die; I cannot escape death. Four, all that is near to me and everyone I love will change— there is no way to escape being separated from them.

Five, I inherit the results of my acts of body, speech and mind; my actions are my continuation.

Looking deeply at each remembrance and breathing in and out with our awareness of each one, we engage our fear in an empowered way. So, after reading his book on fear and this powerful statement, I learned not to fear life and death, and to enjoy every moment with happiness. Awareness of the present moment is of utmost importance in each of our lives. Having said that, I was determined that I was going to get completely well. So, every morning, when I prayed to the Almighty God, I said that I was healing well and I was going to be fine. That feeling became stronger and stronger.

Within two weeks, I met with my neurologist for the first time after my illness. He is a fine physician. After he completed my exam, he gave me one piece of advice, which I regard as golden words. He said, —Whatever you are receiving through the physical therapy or occupational therapy is only 10 percent of it; 90 percent of it, you have to do your homework." That meant I had to keep doing the therapy every day, not counting what I was doing the two to three days a week. I understood what he said and kept doing my therapy every day, no matter how many times a week I was scheduled. This fit in well with my belief, according to the *Bhagavad Gita* (our spiritual book, like the *Bible* and *Koran*), in which it is said you have to do your *karma* (action) in the best way you can without expecting the fruit of the action. As long as you do so, God will take care of the rest. This is one part of Karma Yoga.

I have to tell you about my inquiry into what was the cause of my stroke. I asked all my physicians both in Chicago and back home this question since I am also a medical doctor. None of the physicians gave me a very good answer. In medical terms, they called it a cerebrovascular accident but none of them gave a reason as to what caused the stroke. All my lab work as well as imagings were normal. One physician called it a cryptogenic stroke, which means _cause unknown'. Even though I exercised and took good care of myself, and following proper eating habits, I still ended up with a stroke. The one thing that went through my mind was that _stress' was the main cause of all our sufferings. It was my feeling that the stress I endured during the last three years of my career may have caused it.

Unfortunately, our hospital did not have a speech therapist so I had to get permission from my insurance company to have my speech therapy at another hospital. I talked to a person at the insurance company and she approved 30 sessions of speech therapy in the other hospital. I met the speech therapist for evaluation and she was a wonderful person. I went three days a week for the sessions and her encouragement was very positive. In the beginning, I had a lot of problems remembering numbers and the spellings of words. She gave me homework and encouraged me to do the homework before our next session. I religiously did all my homework, and that really helped build up my confidence. Later on, I was telling her that they should start a stroke support group. She told me that they had had a group before but, for some reason, had discontinued it. I suggested that they restart that group; it would help all of us to gather once a month and exchange our problems and positive things. They started the group again and it was called _Go-Getters, Stroke Support Group'. It was started in the beginning of 2017 and is still going on every month. One other thing I learned from that group is that instead of being called a _stroke patient', you will be called a _stroke survivor'. The word _survivor' gives a very positive feeling that you have regained your physical strength as well as your mental strength. You are getting better physically and mentally every day. Thank God, you are now called a survivor and not as patient!

All my therapies went very well and I religiously followed their recommendations and did my therapies at home, even after all the sessions ended. I still go to the therapy department and do my therapies six days a week on my own.

In September 2016, my son and daughter and their families came to visit me for my 70th birthday. I was elated and enjoyed their visit very much. Also, the son of the Leader of the Gang of Five had gotten married in New Jersey. Due to my stroke, I was unable to attend his wedding. I was the only one among our Gang who was not present at the wedding. My daughter, son-in-law and their children attended their wedding in my absence, which made me very happy. To my surprise, the newlyweds visited our house within a week after their wedding. I was euphoric!

During the fall of 2016, in late October/early November, I was a bit depressed after my family members went home and the therapies ended. I used to have the typical Seasonal Affective Disorder or SAD symptoms throughout my career during fall season as this is the time of year that there is less sunshine and more cold weather. I used to manage this with my daily walking and keeping myself busy in my practice. Most of the time, during my career, I was able to work through them. This time, I was at home not going back to work; I was also not able to walk outside. This was a new experience for me and it was a little rough.

Around this time, we learned from our family in India that my mother-in-law was not doing very well and was having some difficulty in walking. So, we wanted to visit her in the beginning of January 2017. I was hopeful as I was going to travel but as I had not done any traveling since my stroke, I had some self-doubt. However, I made up my mind that I was going to make this trip. We started preparing for the trip to India, and wanted to stay there for six weeks. I was happy that we would escape the bitter winter and I prayed that everything should go well. I will tell you in the next chapter how that trip went and how I felt after that. During this period, I was recovering fairly well except for some weakness in my right arm, especially in my fourth and fifth fingers. The sensation in my right arm and hand was much less in comparison to my left arm and hand. I was able to walk fairly well and my thought process and my speech were almost completely normal. So, I felt very proud of myself, and I felt that going back to my hometown and spending some time with my family would help me to recover faster. Also, I wanted to continue my therapies while I was in India. So, I decided that, once I landed in India, I would seek out a professional guy to help me.

While I was on the road to recovery in the late summer of 2016, my Mentor paid me a visit with another friend. Seeing them in person lifted my spirits sky high. The friend who accompanied him was also a good friend of mine. He is a wonderful human being and a dedicated physician. Both of them were involved in a noble cause to establish a Tamil Chair at Harvard University, Cambridge, Massachusetts. It was a mammoth project, but they had the will power and support of people from all over the world to achieve this noble deed. Later, my Mentor visited me again with his wife. Seeing both of them in person speeded up my recovery much faster. Thank you to them.

Also, after I had returned home, I had had acupuncture treatments administered by one of our family friends, who is a female family doctor. I really appreciated her gentle mannerisms and kindness. That therapy also helped to heal my body. Thank you, my friend.

I want to mention my financial situation since my stroke. I contacted the office supervisor and found out that I had accumulated more than 900 hours of paid sick leave as I had not taken many sick days throughout my past 20 years working for the hospital. So, they assured me I would be financially secure for the next six months. I felt very happy and relieved to hear that good news. Also, I would like to mention how my family physician, who is also my close friend as well as a wonderful person, helped me through this process. In the next chapter, I will tell you my experience while in India.

Chapter Eleven

THE SPIRITUAL JOURNEY TO INDIA AND LATER TO KAUAI; THE FINAL HEALING OF THE BODY AND THE MIND

When you are undecided on which way to turn or what path to follow, remember, there is one who knows and will guide you through every decision and turn in your life; all you have to do is ask, believe you will receive the guidance you want and stay alert to receive your answer. The Supreme Power of the Universe is with you every step you take and all you have to do is rely upon its power and ask.

—The Secret, Daily Teachings, by Rhonda Byrne

That which we affirm constantly has the tendency to take over in our thoughts and to produce changed attitudes.

— Have a Great Day: Daily Affirmations for Positive Living, by Norman Vincent Peale

I was eagerly waiting to make a journey to India in January 2017. I still had some weakness of my right arm as well as my forearm and was experiencing numbness in my right hand. The fine motor movements in my fourth and fifth fingers were still not well coordinated. My right shoulder still had some pain on movement. Knowing these problems, I had decided to find a good physical therapist once I landed in India.

Finally, the day arrived. The weather was cold but there was no snowfall. Luckily, we were able to drive all the way from our town to Chicago, where we stayed overnight and then left the next day.

I must tell you about the winters in our town. When I initially came to this town, we had very cold weather and plenty of snow but, for the last few years, our winters have not been so severe. We have had a few days that are very cold and, though we have snow in the winter, they don't seem to be as bad as before. I think the seasons are changing. It is possibly due to global warming or something else but, definitely, I can see the change.

We took a flight from Chicago to Frankfurt, Germany. It was an eight-hour flight. We had a three-hour layover before flying to India. We landed in Chennai, India after nine hours. We stayed overnight in Chennai and then flew to another town near my place; this took an hour. So, in all, it was almost about a 19-hour journey. I was pretty happy that I had tolerated it well. Initially, I had some concerns, but the journey was comfortable. From there, we took a car and drove almost two-and-a-half hours to our hometown.

By the time we reached our hometown, my mother-in-law was very happy to see us. Unfortunately, she had a problem walking. Before we left for India, after talking to the family, we thought she may have osteoarthritis, which is age-related bone changes. She was a very wonderful human being, and always had a beautiful smile on her face. We called her Annapoorani, who is the goddess of food and nourishment in Hinduism, as she always greeted everyone by serving them food. On this visit, our son also made a visit to our town with his wife and two young children. It was a very brief visit but it made my mother-in-law very happy to see not only her grandson but her great granddaughters as well. They played on her bed, which was a wonderful moment for her. After that, we spent four days with our son and his family in a sea resort for a brief vacation before they flew back to Chicago.

While I was in my native place, resting and enjoying the sunny weather, I found a very wonderful, young and competent physical therapist through my wife's nephew, who is also a physician. He came to our house and I had almost forty minutes of physical therapy every day except Sunday. That was very useful. Thank you so much for the kind referral.

At the time of our visit, the weather was comfortable—close to 70°F every day. It was tropical weather because our town is near the Indian Ocean. The wonderful weather really helped in my healing.

While I was in my hometown, my nephew—who is my eldest brother's oldest son—took me to a few, very old temples in the morning hours. I really enjoyed those outings. Some of the temples are located in small hills, so I had to do some climbing—to my surprise, I was able to do better. That gave me more confidence. So, going to the temples in the mornings and enjoying nature helped me to remember my good old days when I was a young kid and walked to the temple. We traveled by car because of all the vehicles on the road.

After I had successfully enjoyed my vacation in India, I returned to my hometown in Illinois. The weather was much better now. I continued my occupational therapy for a few more weeks until my insurance ran out. Still, I continued to work on all therapies on my own for six days a week. In April 2017, I visited my daughter to attend her first son's fourth birthday. That was the second time we traveled by air. That experience also was pleasant.

After I came back, I was physically and mentally tired. I wanted to get rid of the negative feelings within, so I kept on doing my exercise and reading books and making myself feel better. That summer, our whole family (my children and their families) decided to visit Kauai, Hawaii. There was a famous temple under construction called Iraivan Hindu Temple. We wanted to go and see that place as well. This was my second trip to Kauai: I had first visited the place a couple of years back. This time, we stopped in San Francisco and stayed in my daughter's house for a few days and then flew to Kauai. My son and daughter and their families subsequently joined us.

When I visited the temple, I saw the deity Nataraja. My son reminded me, ―Dad, do you know that this is the one-year anniversary of your medical illness?" Then I realized that it was on July 2, 2016, that I had gotten sick. Now, a year after, I was at the temple worshipping Lord Shiva. Of the many names Shiva had, there is one form we call Nataraja—it means he is in the dancing posture; the dance is called Shiva Thandavam in Tamil. According to Hindu mythology, Shiva is Brahman, or the unmanifested form. When Brahman creates, he transforms into Shakti. Here Shiva is in the dancing form. When I was looking at that deity, I was reminded of a line by Eckhart Tolle in his book, *A New Earth*: ―Life is the dancer and I am the dance." There is a presence inside you that is the life force/the Creator/the dancer, and you are the dance. When the life force exits from you, the dance ends. When the presence/life force enters another being, the dance continues.

When we visited the temple, *puja* was going on— this was good timing and I really enjoyed it. When I was in the temple, my mind became very clear. I was thinking about what I was going to do. For the past forty years, I had been a medical doctor, healing a lot of innocent young kids. In that process, I had made money and fame. Now after the illness, I was confused as to whether to go back and start all over again or be born again and start a new avatar. After visiting the temple, my mind was very clear. I said to myself, ―This is it. I am going to retire from my previous avatar or journey as a doctor. I am going to start a new life". I felt much better and happier.

When I went back to my hometown, I told my family about my decision and they happily accepted it. So, I met with my hospital's CEO and gave him 90 days' notice, which is routine for any corporate position. After I gave him the letter, I felt very good and I knew I was going to be fine. For some reason, the Almighty has shown me a new path but to get to that path he gave me a good lesson (the stroke). I took it as a positive thing that I had to go through this for one year.

Chapter Twelve

I AM THAT I AM

Self-transformation is not just about changing yourself.
It means shifting yourself to a complete new dimension
of experience and perception.

When sounds are in tune, they become music; out of
tune, they become noise. It is the same thing with you.
When all aspects of you are in tune, you become music;
out of tune, you become noise.

Confusion is better than stupid conclusions. In
confusion, there is still a possibility. In stupid
conclusion, there is no possibility.

—Sadhguru

If you did not have love in you, you could not be alive
and exist as a human being. If you removed all the
layers that are wrapped around you, peeling them off
one by one, you would be left with an eternal light of
consciousness that is made of pure love. Life's journey

entails peeling away the layers until you reach that core of you which is absolute love.

—Rhonda Byrne

After my joyful get together with my loving kids and grandkids at Kauai, Hawaii, in July 2017, I returned home. I started walking outside, enjoying the sunshine. I had given my 90-day letter of resignation from my job, and I was feeling very peaceful at this point. In October 2017, the hospital gave me a nice retirement party; as a gift, they gave me a wristwatch that was engraved with my years of service as a pediatrician. In the fall of 2017, my office staff gave me a wonderful send-off party, and a nice pocket watch as a gift. I felt the warmth of love and affection from all my fellow staff members.

At this point, I was feeling much better but changed. My energy level was gradually getting lower, and I became more anxious, sometimes even depressed. Occasionally, I even had some suicidal thoughts. *Oh, that's not good!* Usually doctors get more stressed out because of the job, and I had heard that suicide rates among physicians are very high. My god, I did not want to join that group! At this point, I continued my daily walking and going to physical therapy. I tried to keep myself more active but my feelings of depression and occasional suicidal thoughts, as well as my low energy level, were persistent. This was the beginning of fall, so I thought this was the Seasonal Affective Disorder or SAD I had experienced previously throughout my practice—but, this time, it was a little bit different.

In late October, our Indian community had the Diwali annual function. My Birth Mate came from Chicago with his wife to attend the event. I sang at the function. I am a singer—not a very good singer, but I used to sing. My Birth Mate, a music genius, performed two songs. It was a wonderful evening. After he left, my loneliness and feelings of losing my mind kept popping up. *Was I losing my mind?* I always thought I was the master and the mind was my servant, but things were changing.

Later, I realized that our thought process was wrong. Recently, there was an opioid crisis in the United States, and a lot of people were getting addicted. I always thought once you surrendered to your mind, it took over and created a lot of negative thoughts such as a hatred, jealousy, anger, greed, lust and even drug addiction. That is a compulsive desire and not a conscious choice. So, knowing all these things and being a physician, I decided that I would never surrender to my mind! I was going to take charge.

At this time, I went to Chicago for two days to see my son and his family. We drove all the way from my hometown and, after I reached his house, I was very quiet and silent, like a dead man. My son said, ―Dad, are you tired? You don‛t look right. Are you depressed? You better see your doctor and take some medication. I don‛t want you to be like this." That struck me hard— even my son was telling me that something is going on. So, after I went home, I saw my personal physician, who is also my good friend, and told him about my low energy, feeling of loneliness and depression. However, because of my pride, I did not tell him about the suicidal thoughts. You know, that is one of the things that doctors will always hide from other doctors—and it creates a lot of problems in the later part of their life. He told me —You are fine. You are healthy. You are improving and your vitals are great. You don't need any medication." Usually, this kind of low energy will gradually go away by the time the season changes, so I went home with the thought that I was going to be fine. To tell the truth, I still felt very lonely and unable to do anything. I felt like I was in prison and not able to come out. It is okay to be alone, but it is not okay to feel lonely.

At this time, a friend of mine, who lives in Chicago, invited me and my wife to attend his daughter's wedding. The marriage was held the first weekend in November. He was the one who taught me philosophy, when I was at St. Xavier's College in India for the pre-university course before I joined medical school. I always liked him. He had recently retired and was living in Chicago. During our conversation, he told me that he had also suffered a stroke, which had affected his speech, and had had chronic back problems. He then told me that he was doing something different—now, he could walk on the treadmill for almost five miles every day and was doing very well. He told me he was doing yoga and meditation; that he had found a guru and felt a lot better. I said, —What is this guru nonsense? You know, all the gurus are fake. They take a lot of money from your pocket and leave you in the desert. When I come for the wedding, I will talk to you in person about that." In the meantime, I was slowly losing interest in religion. I never liked conditioned religion. I knew the Power (my Amman in me); I knew there was a God. I was never an atheist but I was becoming agnostic. I knew there was something beyond us but I did not know how to connect with that Power. So, I was really confused at this point. I thought, maybe, a guru might help me. The thought of reaching out to a genuine guru had been in my mind for a long time but it was now popping up more and more, especially after the conversation with my friend. If I did find a genuine guru, would he be able to guide me to the right path?

Finally, the day came for us to attend the wedding. A couple of my medical school classmates from different parts of the United States, as well as my friend from Galesburg, came for the wedding. It was a very nice reunion among old classmates. My Birth Mate as well as my Think Tank attended the wedding and we had a chance to see each other and have a very nice chat. The wedding day was very beautiful. It was cold and windy—typical of Chicago weather in November. The wedding venue was well decorated and there was a large picture of a person, placed behind where the bride and bridegroom were seated. I looked at that picture. The one thing that really attracted me were the person's powerful eyes; he wore a turban and had a long white beard. Looking at the picture, I felt I might know this person. Maybe I had seen his picture. I found out that he was called Sadhguru.

During the reception, I was talking to the bride's father and asked him how he was feeling. He said, "I'm feeling a lot better. I am so happy, I have a lot of energy and I am doing daily meditation—that is helping me. I have found a very positive guru, and he has made me a very positive and productive person." I did not buy into his ideas. Again, I was less receptive about gurus and made fun of them. He suggested that I get to know him through a program called "Inner Engineering"—an online program. That way, I would be able to find out what it was all about. He added, "Kesavan, do not believe anything I say. Don't believe all the books you have read so far. Go with an open mind—be a seeker." I asked, "What do you mean by seeker?" He said, "Seeker means trying to explore with an open mind, to find out the truth by yourself. You don't have to believe the guru I follow. You can ask him if you have a doubt. If you go with the mentality of a seeker, you will find out."

I was still unreceptive to his notion. Later on, my friend from Galesburg joined the conversation; he had already taken a few courses from Inner Engineering. The next morning, before leaving for our hometown, we had breakfast with my Think Tank and his wife. I was telling them about the conversation I had had the previous night with the bride's father. My Think Tank told me he was also looking for a guru. He has visited many gurus but, still, he was not totally convinced. His wife was also very negative. So, I told my Think Tank and his wife, ―Why don't we explore this possibility with an open mind, with no preformed judgment? The bride's father told me this guru has the Isha Institute of Inner-Sciences in McMinnville, Tennessee. We could just go and see it. Why don't we make a visit to that place in the summer of 2018? We will just go there for fun. We don't have to believe anything or follow his teaching, just go there for fun as a summer trip with our wives." He said that was a good idea. His wife added, ―Well, Kesavan, that is a good idea. I think we should do that."

On the way back to our home, my wife and I visited a Hindu temple in Aurora, Illinois. This temple is called Sri Venkateswara (Balaji) Temple. I liked this temple. When I came out after worship, I met the priest, whom I have known for a long time. He asked, ―Doctor, how are you? Are you doing well? Are you working?" I said I was not working. He told me that it was better if I continued working and kept up my routine. ―Once you don't follow your early morning routine, you will become tired and you will become lazier. So, please don't give up," he added. I thought to myself that I had already retired from my profession. I wanted to do something different, take on a different journey, and here he was, talking about the routine. After I had had my stroke, and during my recovery time, I usually got up a bit later in the morning, around six-thirty or seven a.m., which was very late when I was working. I was taking things easier and I enjoyed it but I did feel I was becoming lazier. I decided that I should get up early, as I had done before. Maybe I should start my day earlier, as it was my DNA from a young age. I was thinking about this when we returned home.

I always have had faith in the Infinite Power that is working through me—my Amman, or my Shakti. I believe that we all need religion to understand the Infinite Power but religion is just like a bridge, so that you can cross the river. Once you cross over the bridge, you don't have to look back. You need to connect with the ultimate Infinite Power that is within you to become spiritual. However, on connecting that dot, I was still not very clear; I was just hanging on. The very next day, my Galesburg friend called me and said, —Kesavan, are you still interested in listening to the introduction to Inner Engineering online by Sadhguru? I have a discount coupon. If you are not interested, I can send it to somebody else." Initially, I was very hesitant about accepting his offer. Eventually, I agreed and said I would look into it even though I had no idea of what I was getting into. He sent me the coupon for the free course introduction. Thank you, my friend.

The next morning, I got up at four a.m., as I had done when I was in active practice and during my younger days. After brushing my teeth, I sat in front of my computer and listened to the introduction course to Inner Engineering. It took about 45 minutes. A nice young man appeared on the screen and started the introduction course. Almost immediately, I realized that he was answering a lot of questions that I was grappling with. *My god, this was SOMETHING I had been looking for*. So, at the end of the introduction course, I knew that I wanted to complete the seven courses of the Inner Engineering. Of course, I had to pay for the course, but it was not big money. I could take it within a week or two weeks, a month or even six months—there was no time limit. After I finished all seven courses online, if I was interested, I would have to attend the final session for the Inner Engineering Completion Program with Sadhguru or his teachers. On a few occasions, Sadhguru would be there and, in his presence, we could do the final one. It all sounded very positive. I got up early for seven days and did the course. In between, I was really sick with a cold for one day, but that did not deter me from listening to the course. After successfully finishing the seven courses, I felt very relieved. My anxiety, depression and suicidal thoughts were gone, and I had much more energy. Every morning after I did that course, I took a shower and went to the hospital, where I walked on the treadmill. In fact, to my surprise, I was able to do the treadmill for almost 40 minutes, without even holding onto the bar. I was having so much energy and was feeling very happy. Then, I found a very interesting book written by Sadhguru which was a *New York Times* bestseller—it was called *Inner Engineering: A Yogi's Guide to Joy*. I got the book through Amazon and I started reading it. In the meantime, I contacted my Think Tank over the phone and told him about my experience and feelings. I told him that I could send him an email about this Inner Engineering; if he was interested, he could take the course. He said that was a good idea. So, he enrolled in the Introduction and subsequently finished the Inner Engineering course online.

These are the five things I learned from the course. Number one: Desire is natural, not compulsive but conscious, and awareness is the freedom to choose. Number two: Being responsible and responsibility is not limited by boundaries but the action is limited. The mind creates the boundary." Number three: Seeing the moment of inevitability and being able to accept it as it is. Number four: Knowing that I am not the body; I am not even the mind. That creates a space between you and the body and the mind. Number five: The most important—knowing about karma/action (cause and effect). That means being responsible for your own karma and its effect and not blaming it on others. By doing daily meditation, we develop awareness within: (1) I am/self—love and kindness; (2) My life—being compassionate and caring to one another; (3) To the world—show true empathy to fellow human beings and give unconditional love. I liked that concept of living— being alive and being conscious.

Now, I wondered if I did need a guru, one who could guide me to the right path. According to Sadhguru, the guru is like a live road map, like a GPS, and that was the image I could relate to most—not a patriarchal messiah or card-holding member of the spiritual elect, but just a map, a path, willing to be worn and abraded by the footprints of hundreds of thousands of travelers eager to make their journey home. I liked that concept. I also liked the way Sadhguru described our mind in his book, *Inner Engineering: A Yogi's Guide to Joy*. In the yogic system of classifications, the mind has sixteen dimensions, which fall into four categories. Intellect is the discerning, or discriminatory, dimension of the mind (in Sanskrit, it is called *buddhi*). The accumulative dimension of the mind, or memories (*manas*), which gathers information. Awareness (*chitta*) is beyond both intellect and memory, which is pure intelligence. The fourth dimension is called *ahankara* and this is your sense of identity.

After I went through that seven-day course of Inner Engineering, I started doing daily meditation called Isha Kriya in the early morning. *Isha* means that which is the source of creation; *Kriya* means an inward action towards that. The meditation lasts about 15 minutes and gives me a lot of relief.

In the meantime, I wanted to fulfill my longtime desire to write my memoir, so I started dictating through audio about my experiences. Since I was not able to write as clearly as before my stroke, I found a wonderful human being, a good transcriptionist, who helped me write my memoir. I am eternally grateful for her kindness and compassion. Christmas was approaching and we were planning to make a visit to India in the early part of January 2018. Also, my Think Tank and my Birth Mate decided to make a visit to

India at that time as well, and I was excited about that. I was very happy that we could be back in India together.

Before I planned to visit India, I surprised my Birth Mate by sending him a copy of *Inner Engineering: A Yogi's Guide to Joy* by Sadhguru. He received the book shortly after I left for India but before his departure to India. My Think Tank left for India a couple of days before my departure. In the meantime, my friend from Galesburg also traveled to India at approximately the same time; while he was there, he made a courteous visit to my hometown, specifically to see my mother-in-law. This genuine gesture of kindness by my friend made her feel very happy. Also, my Think Tank and my Birth Mate, whom she knew, visited her while they were in India. These kind acts on their part also made my mother-in-law very happy. Thank you all so much for your love and affection.

While in India, my routine included visiting the temples in the early morning. As mentioned earlier, most of the temples are in the hills so I made this my early morning walk. This time, I went to the temples all by myself. The weather was perfect, close to the 70°F in the early morning, then going up to 90°F by the afternoon. I really enjoyed the tropical climate. I also continued my routine of getting up in the early morning and doing a yoga routine called Surya Namaskar (sun salutation)—12 rounds of breathing and stretching, which I did very regularly. After this, I showered, did my Isha Kriya meditation and then visited the temples.

Even though we encountered some small issues throughout our days in India, because of my daily meditation and yoga, all was well by the end of each day.

While in India, we had a college reunion of our old classmates from our medical school. We gathered in a place nearby my town, in a backwater resort. Out of the original 200 in our class, about 35 of our classmates came with their families, and we had a wonderful time. My Birth Mate came along with me but my Think Tank had already returned to the United States before the reunion.

While my Birth Mate was in India, he was staying in our town and I met with him a few times. He conveyed to me that he was very happy that I gave him the book, *Inner Engineering*. He had started reading the book during his flight to India; it really piqued his interest and excited him. He even relayed to me that he was going to take the Inner Engineering courses and enrolled in them before he went back to the United States.

So, after our wonderful stay in India, we returned back to Chicago on February 17, 2018, and drove back to our house the same day.

My Birth Mate, my Think Tank and I were planning to attend the Inner Engineering session with Sadhguru in Philadelphia in May. I still had not thought about him as my guru; I was still searching. As Sadhguru always says, ─Do not believe everything you hear or read, always seek the truth". So, I would seek and find out the truth, and just leave it that way.

I also learned through his teaching that we always talk about stress, and about stress management. Sadhguru said that it is not about managing the stress but about how you deal with the stress that is the important point. Just like it is not about money. When money is in the pocket, it is okay as long as it is not getting into your mind. The idea of having money or having stress is not the one you have to be anxious or stressed about—it is all about how you deal with it. After taking the Inner Engineering course and listening to his lectures, I learned more about the meaning of the inner being, the life energy. Let me explain this in a simple way. We have our body as an outer compartment and we have a subtle mind as a part of that compartment. The mind has four different dimensions—intellect, *ahankara*, *manas* and *chitta*/pure intelligence. We have an inner compartment that is subtle and is pure consciousness. That pure consciousness is our life energy. This is a highly spiritual concept. The pure consciousness/self finally surrenders to the universal consciousness, the Creator—then you attain nirvana and feel the absolute eternal bliss that is union with the Divinity. That is, I Am That I Am'.

I am stress-free on most days now. I have no fear, I am not anxious and my energy levels are always up. My happiness or inner joy is almost balanced and I am trying to keep my mind in the present most of the time.

Now, I am becoming the ‗Chinna Thambi‗, which is what my brothers called me in my younger days. This means ‗little brother‗—a carefree, joyful and fearless soul. Now, I feel this is very true. I am healthy both physically and mentally and I have the energy to carry on. Now, I am going on a different path that is more spiritual. After passing through the religious bridge, I am not looking back and I don‗t need that bridge anymore. As Eckhart Tolle says in his book *New Earth*, life is the dancer and I am the dance. I believe what he says.

Also, gratitude is very important—giving thanks and having appreciation for everything we have every day, every moment and living mindfully at the present moment. Also, we have to be kind to every fellow human being. We must also be thankful to the Infinite Intelligence, the Great Almighty, who blessed us so much. So, appreciation, gratitude, kindness and universal love are the basic things we have to develop in our journey. I also learned from my whole experience that you have to have a dream, you have to believe the dream and you have to follow the dream. Throughout your journey, you have the Divine Presence within you. Once you realize the ‗presence‗ of that divinity, you develop confidence as well as great inner strength. So, looking back at my whole life, I was blessed. I had divine blessing, I had a dream and I am following through with the dream.